MIRACLE MAPLES

MIRACLE MAPLES

T.C. Cameron

Palmetto Publishing Group
Charleston, SC

Miracle Maples
Copyright © 2018 by T.C. Cameron
All rights reserved

First Edition

Printed in the United States

ISBN 13: 978-1-64111-194-2
ISBN-10: 1-64111-194-1

TABLE OF CONTENTS

FOREWORD

By Marty Budner

SPRING SIGNALS NEW LIFE. FRESH HOPE. RENEWED OPTIMISM.

A group of energetic teenagers from Birmingham took that spring fever to the ultimate level in 1988.

For one month, Seaholm High School's varsity baseball team surged to historic heights and took the Birmingham community to a new degree of delirium with an improbable state tournament run.

The end result was a Class A championship.

The Maples went on an incredible postseason roll, winning seven straight playoff games and 16 overall en route to the school's first – and still only – baseball championship.

But, it's not just the victories that characterized this particular title chase. It's the way the wins were achieved. The Maples, you see, won five straight games in their last turn at-bat. They trailed in that final turn in three of those games. In both regional games, they needed to score to force extra innings. They needed a miraculous fielder's choice play just to reach the regional championship.

In each instance, they showed unbelievable courage and determination. Seaholm hosted state-ranked Southfield-Lathrup in the pre-district opener at Maple Field. They rallied to register the 3-2 upset victory.

That was only the beginning. In the district doubleheader a few days later at Royal Oak's Memorial Park, Seaholm defeated neighborhood rival Birmingham Brother Rice (2-1) and captured the district title with a win over Troy (3-2). Again, the Maples found a way to win both games by scoring the winning run in their last turn at the plate.

The momentum created by Seaholm's stirring victories started to take a stranglehold on the area. The two-game regional tournament was next. Could they keep it up? Could they sustain their success? Could they add even more postseason hardware to their school's trophy cases?

Seaholm next traveled out of Oakland County where its journey continued to unfold.

The Maples went to Grosse Pointe North High School in Wayne County and a pair of recorded extra-inning wins, beating East Detroit (7-6) in nine innings and Warren Mott (13-10) in eight innings, a game that took three days to complete.

By now, Seaholm's postseason truly turned magical. The Maples had soared to the Final Four and the community's fascination flew right along with them. Ironically, the Final Four, played at Michigan State's Kobs Field, proved almost anti-climatic compared to what had happened in their previous five games. Seaholm won its final two games by a combined seven runs. The Maples won their first five games by that same total.

In the semifinal, Seaholm easily defeated Port Huron (7-2) to qualify for the program's first ever state championship game. The Maples then took down Taylor Kennedy (11-9) to claim the improbable title. Seaholm proved a team of destiny, but, like all successful tourney runs, you have to catch a few breaks along the way. Seaholm received a major break in the championship game when it didn't have to face Kennedy's All-State pitcher Steve Avery who had already reached his allotted amount of innings pitched per week and could not take the mound against the Maples.

Seaholm achieved the title under their unassuming, quiet, but well-respected head coach Don Sackett. Assisted by his son Mark and

Andy Little, Sackett emerged as the perfect leader of the talented team filled with depth and balance. Sackett seemed to make every right move and the players responded to his veteran coaching in championship style. They believed in each other, their system and their resiliency.

Matt Newton supplied brilliant pitching and raw emotion. Mike Carroll provided top-flight catching and solid leadership. Todd Siefken, Chris Kauth and Todd Glandt were other inspirational leaders.

Whether cherished or disdained, high school experiences are forever etched in the annals of everyone's memory bank. Although it's been 30 years since that amazing Michigan High School Athletic Association state championship, the 'Miracle Maples' from Seaholm remain forever an integral part of Birmingham's folklore.

It's a safe bet you'll have as much fun reading about their remarkable journey as the players had celebrating their unprecedented success that spring.

— Marty Budner
Hometown Life

ACKNOWLEDGEMENTS

FOR THE LAST DECADE, I'VE LIVED IN ANNAPOLIS, MARYLAND, 575 miles from Birmingham and Seaholm High School. Much of the information, historical facts and details within this book was discovered via the Internet, email or by telephone.

My favorite moment writing this book occurred in Baltimore, at Oriole Park at Camden Yards. I can't recall who the Birds were playing or what the score was, but because they lost a franchise-record 115 games in 2018, Baltimore was likely losing when the letters "SEA" popped up on the out-of-town scoreboard. My 11-year-old daughter, Brooklyn (named for the Dodgers), pointed and said with absolute confidence, "Look Dad, there's the score for Seaholm!"

It's easy to forget the massive amounts of time sacrificed at the altar of writing, a true labor of love. Brooklyn, thank you for allowing me the time to finish this project. Thank you for reminding me to take some time for summer. Thank you for allowing baseball to be a big part of our lives.

To everyone else, I offer my sincere thanks for your invaluable assistance:

To Michelle E. Woodward, my research assistant, thank you for your encouragement and willingness to help while pouring through an endless stream of news clips and yearbook pages at libraries in Birmingham and Royal Oak.

To Erin Sackett, thank you for lending your design skill and keen eye in presenting the front and back cover and spine for *Miracle Maples*. Welcome to your new family.

To the subjects of this title, Birmingham Seaholm, the 1988 Class A champions, thank you for graciously sharing your story — good and bad — within these pages more than 30 years after it happened. Former math teacher and baseball coach Don Sackett, Mike Carroll, Crede Colgan, Jeff Fertuck, Todd Glandt, Chris Kauth, Cam Mueller, Matt Newton, Steve Sheckell, Todd Seifken and Bill Stephenson.

From Royal Oak Kimball, the 1988 SMA champions, Hall of Fame coach Frank Clouser and the Knights' Steve Kinkade.

Thank you to Seaholm graduate and former assistant coach Mark Sackett, for answering my endless stream of phone calls, texts and emails. To Mark's better half, Linda Sackett, thank you for opening your home to Michelle and I. The face-to-face interviews we conducted and artwork acquired would not be possible without you.

From *Hometown Life* — formerly known in Birmingham as the *Observer & Eccentric* newspaper — reporter and editor Marty Budner, who coined the "Miracle Maples" name and Dan Dean, former *Observer & Eccentric* photographer and now managing editor of *Hometown Life*. This title is simply not possible without this great newspaper's assistance.

From the now-closed *Daily Tribune* in Royal Oak, reporter and columnist Jim Evans, and former Executive Sports Editor Steve Stein. Thanks to *Detroit Free Press* publisher Paul Bhatia and administrative assistant Theresa Oakes.

Coaches and administrators from many Michigan high schools contributed layers of stats, information and context needed to recreate this story. My apologies if I have missed anyone. Aaron Frank, Birmingham Seaholm athletic director; current Royal Oak High School baseball coach and former Seaholm baseball coach Greg Porter; Brian Gordon, former Kimball and Royal Oak High School Hall of Fame baseball coach and athletic director; Loren Ristovski, Taylor High School athletic director, formerly athletic director at Hamtramck High School and Taylor Kennedy High School; Gregg P. Wagner, Port Huron High School athletic director and assistant principal.

From the Michigan High School Athletic Association, Executive Director Mark Uyl and Communications Director John Johnson.

From the 2018 World Champion Boston Red Sox, General Manager David Dombrowski and Media Director Kevin Gregg; Danny Schmitz, head baseball coach at Bowling Green State University; Tim Hepler from Eastern Michigan University; Camron Ghorbi from the University of Miami; Kristin Keirns from Western Michigan University; Elisa Mitton from the University of Windsor; Justin Seidler from Albion College.

Helping us with the arduous task of researching scores, game stories and profiles, spell-checking first and last names from newspapers and yearbooks as well as confirming employment and graduation records of teachers, coaches and student-athletes was an invaluable army of media and human resource professionals.

Elisabeth 'Elly' Phou, Ethan Cronkite and Vicki Sower from the Baldwin Public Library in Birmingham; Susan File from Birmingham Public Schools; Shirley Atcho from Hazel Park Public Schools; Matthew Day and Melanie Nielsen from the Royal Oak Public Library; Toni Isaac at the Troy High School library; Elizabeth Thornburg from the Troy Historical Society; Gail Cram from Eastpointe High School; Staci Vought at Troy Athens High School.

Paula Sutterfield from Royal Oak Public Schools; Principal James Mio from Royal Oak Shrine High School; Christine Renner from the National Shrine of the Little Flower Basilica; Steve Wejroch from the Archdiocese of Detroit.

Thank you to East Detroit High School graduate and fellow Eastern Michigan University classmate Paul Nucci– for helping me

ID the 1988 East Detroit Shamrocks. Eastpointe? Nah, it's still East Detroit to me.

Finally, to Gavin Christie of Birmingham, who sacrificed the use of the microfiche reader in the Baldwin Public Library: your kindness did not go unnoticed.

DEDICATION

ON JUNE 28, 2018, AT 2:33 P.M., A SICK AND DEEPLY TROUBLED man blasted his way through the glass security door at the *Capital Gazette* newspaper in Annapolis, Md. His ire was directed at the paper's commitment to shining light on this man's darkest behaviors, while giving voice to the plight of the woman he consistently harassed.

The intimate, harrowing details shared by those who experienced this massacre — including the panic of trying to survive and the last acts and words of the five who didn't — continue to haunt. In the days and weeks to follow, the staff from "The Cap" who survived the attack pressed on, making deadline that day and every day since.

If you didn't understand or appreciate the resolve that comes with the mission of newspapering, you have to acknowledge and respect it now.

I worked at the *Capital Gazette* from August of 2009 until July of 2015. I'm proud to call myself an alumnus of this newsgathering organization. When the paper was purchased by the *Baltimore Sun* in 2014, I was part of an amazing group of people who helped move the paper's physical location from 2000 Capital Drive to 888 Bestgate, transitioning the publication from an afternoon daily into morning delivery and produce the paper within a new platform.

The newspapers I've been a part of provided outstanding content while upholding the fundamental principles of journalism. They include the *Ann Arbor News*, the *Oakland Press* (Pontiac, Mich.) and the *Daily Tribune* (Royal Oak, Mich.) and the *Capital-Gazette* (Annapolis, Md.).

Newspapers serve an essential function, reporting and cataloging the life and times of those who make our cities and towns notable and newsworthy. Without the archived work found in physical and on-line repositories of sportswriters, photographers and editors from the *Observer & Eccentric* and *Daily Tribune*, and larger metro dailies like the *Detroit Free Press* and *Detroit News*, this title would not be possible.

Miracle Maples is dedicated to the spirit and mission of the light newspapers provide like a beacon from a lighthouse at publications large and small, across America and around the globe.

— *T.C. Cameron*

After being purchased by the Baltimore Sun Media Group, employees of the Capital-Gazette newspaper in Annapolis, Md. said farewell to the paper's former headquarters in August, 2014. The paper's operations moved to Bestgate Road. On June 28, 2018, an unimaginable tragedy unfolded in a matter of minutes. Photo by Paul Gillespie

CHAPTER ONE:

A POISON TREE

"FUCK THIS SHIT! I'M OUT OF HERE!"

Mike Carroll, Birmingham Seaholm's 16-year-old catcher, was enraged. During the last home game of the 1987 season, his stubborn-as-a-mule coach, Don Sackett, was replacing him, turning a long-simmering argument turned into a full scale blow-up. Carroll angrily packed his mitt, bat and all his catching gear into his bag and began storming towards the end of the dugout close to third base. That's when Sackett tossed another barb at his catcher: "Don't let the door hit you where the Lord split you."

Without breaking stride or turning his head, Carroll volleyed back: "Fuck you too, coach!"

Now he marched past Seaholm's parents and students above the dugout and along the third base foul line. In front of a row of neighboring homes, "The Hill" is where everyone from Seaholm assembles to watch the Maples play. The game stood still for the ugly spectacle. Umpires watched with besmirched faces — what sports official hasn't wanted to tell a coach what this 16-year-old said at least once? — while Troy's bench cackled with laughter.

As he escaped the view of the field and approached the parking lot, Carroll was intercepted by Doug Fraser, Seaholm's new football coach. A young, energetic do'er who had previously built up the program at Lake Orion High School, Fraser was gregarious and personable — tough in the moment — and never mistaken for an overzealous disciplinarian.

Seeing a student-athlete in distress, Fraser pled with Carroll to stop and talk but the new coach's ears were scorched with more jet blast.

Football coach Doug Fraser came to Seaholm from Lake Orion in 1987.

"Fuck Sackett and fuck this place! I'm through!" Carroll screamed. Fraser asked him point-blank: "Mike, are you sure you want to end your career this way?" Carroll thundered back: "I don't fucking care! Leave me the hell alone — go play Godfather to someone who cares!"

An eeriness hung over the game's final nine outs after play resumed. Lacking an eligible substitute for the rest of the day, Seaholm lost, 11-4. Troy had taken mercy on the Maples by taking no extra bases after Carroll's incident as Seaholm waved feebly in their final two turns at bat.

"I remember all this shit going down in the dugout, Sackett and Carroll holding their ground until Carroll gave that ultimatum and walked away," Siefken said. "We all looked at each other and said, 'What the fuck just happened — it this real? — Carroll actually quit?' It was disappointing because Carroll was respected among the team. It was not one of the finer moments for Seaholm baseball."

After the post-game handshake, Seaholm's players got the field cleaned up in silence. Sackett said nothing and showed no emotion, but internally he was steamed. The parents meanwhile buzzed incessantly. One parent in particular was beyond disappointed. Frank Sheckell, father to Seaholm basketball star Steve Sheckell, had been one of Carroll's little league coaches. He didn't see Sackett's old-school coaching principles colliding with new-age philosophies of a teenager. In Frank Sheckell's eyes, Carroll's actions were unacceptable.

"Steve and I weren't super close in school, but when I found out how upset his Dad was, it cemented the frost in our relationship," Carroll said. "It's the reason Sheck and I aren't overly friendly today."

In the coach's locker room, away from din of the field, Sackett found peace. *These know-it-all kids know everything...just ask them,*" he thought to himself as he pulled his uniform off. "*Maybe it's best Carroll is gone...*"

The quiet was disturbed by the phone ringing. It was Steve Stein from Royal Oak's *Daily Tribune*. Determined not to air out Seaholm's dirty laundry in Royal Oak's paper, Sackett relayed just the bare minimum of details. Before he hung up, he asked Stein if he had any other scores. Among others, Stein told him Kimball had clinched the SMA title. Sackett let out an audible sigh and thought to himself: "*Kimball... Of course they did.*"

With one game to go, Sackett wondered, "*How much worse could it get?*" as he hung up his uniform. This question was rooted all the way back to tryouts, when Seaholm's 1987 season fell apart before it started. High school baseball tryouts are an insufferable time to be outside in Michigan. Snow mingles with rain and gusty winds. It's rare to receive two days in a row of playable weather and not uncommon for your school's field to get just a day or two of prep before the season's first game. At most schools in Michigan, preseason practices take place in the gymnasium.

When Sackett had selected his 15 players, Dave Martin wasn't one of them. After a year on the freshman team, Martin spent the next two years on varsity. He could catch and play the outfield, serviceable but unspectacular at both. Since 1985, primary catching duties belonged to Carroll. Junior varsity coach Andy Little urged Sackett to move Carroll, then a freshman, up to varsity after he'd played a handful of games.

"We knew he wouldn't hit the senior pitchers he would face, but there was no doubt he was our program's best catcher," Little said.

Now a senior, Martin's role was a backup catcher and a bit of a nomad anywhere else on the field. This was proven to Sackett during a 1986 game at Southfield when Martin was playing right field. He lost a tooth when he awkwardly crashed into a metal support pole of the fence chasing a long fly ball.

"I was playing centerfield, trying to call him off, but he never pulled back," Chris Kauth recalls. "His tooth didn't just break, it disintegrated into powder."

Sackett's reputation for playing his best players exclusively was well-known. It was one of the reasons his teams suffered attrition. Reserves sat and atrophied, less motivated to stick around when spring's warmth arrived. But besides Sackett's belief that Martin would have a difficult time finding any playing time, Martin didn't make the team because they didn't like one another. None of this information was known when Sackett listed the final roster. He didn't explain to anyone why they did or didn't make the team, a holdover protocol from 1964 when Sackett took over the program.

"There was no junior varsity or freshman teams back then, so I'd get 150-200 guys coming out for the baseball team," Sackett said. "I couldn't tell each kid individually why they had been cut because we had so many kids trying out."

Sackett closed the gym and went home. He wasn't inside from the garage five minutes when the phone rang. Henry Martin was on the other end, asking why his son had been cut from the team. After explaining the likely lack of playing time, Sackett offered statistical evidence from the previous season to validate his decision.

Sackett understood the elder Martin's angst but reminded himself, *"I'm trying to win and I need the very best players I can find. I can't be worried about hurt feelings."*

In Sackett's mind, the decision was sound, reasoned and final. But like street signs, lawyers are found on every corner in Birmingham and Henry Martin didn't have to look long or far to find someone to help him fight. The following Monday morning, when Sackett arrived at Seaholm athletic director Dick Rosenthal's office to turn in his final roster, his boss was waiting for him. He told Sackett to hold on to the document and be prepared to attend a meeting that afternoon. The topic? Why Dave Martin had been cut from the team.

Internally, Sackett was incredulous. *"Why do I have to justify this decision again? I made it on my own. I explained it to Henry Martin. Now I have to justify it to you, too? I never told you who you should pick for your swim teams. You hired me to be coach, pick the team and make the decisions. Leave me the hell alone."*

But Rosenthal hadn't hired Sackett; he'd inherited him when he became athletic director. Before moving into administration, Rosenthal had been Seaholm's boys' swim coach, and his teams won the SMA five times and finished second four times. His 1982 team, the Class A runner-up at the state championship meet, came within hundreths of a second of dethroning Ann Arbor Pioneer, the state's dominant swimming power in the late 1970s and early 1980s. He was named state coach of the year in 1976, won the Matt Mann Award for outstanding contribution to swimming in 1982 and had coached over 30 high school All-Americans. In 1994, Rosenthal was inducted into the Michigan High School Coaches' Association's Hall of Fame.

No one doubted Rosenthal's swimming pedigree, but in this situation, Sackett saw his boss as a fish out of water.

The conference room quickly filled with eagles that afternoon. Rosenthal and Henry Martin, Martin's attorney and a union representative were already present when Sackett entered the room. Also present was Seaholm principal Jim Wallendorf, who chaired Seaholm's math department and taught before becoming principal. Wallendorf was Sackett's friend, but he wasn't there to defend the optics of cutting a senior after three years in the program. This wasn't a discussion, it was a referendum on a coach's decision, and his immediate superiors would cast the deciding votes.

Almost immediately, Sackett started to seethe, and he thought of the one person he knew didn't have to put up with this show.

"I'll bet Frank Clouser doesn't have to put up with this kind of shit…"

He was right. Clouser, Kimball's highly-successful coach — and Sackett's primary coaching rival — could cut seniors. At Kimball, juniors were expected to show what they could do in non-league games and doubleheaders. If you didn't perform or got passed by younger players as a senior, Clouser could cut you. He always played a healthy stable of juniors, too, so his teams were never caught empty-handed.

"Like every other coach, I had parents who sent letters to my athletic director and principal complaining about why their kid wasn't playing, etc., but my administration supported my policies because I was upfront with them and the kids," Clouser said. "High school sports isn't a city recreation league. We were trying to win, not create playing time for each kid on the team."

Sackett wanted to win, too, even if he wasn't as driven as his Royal Oak rival. By agreeing to Henry Martin's request for a meeting, Rosenthal and Wallendorf delivered a awful civics lesson: if you don't earn your way on merit, seek your outcome by threatening legal action. Moreover, micromanaging the coach undercut the coach's authority, a premise later cemented in Sackett's mind by the Carroll implosion.

"I saw the people in that room lining up against me, so against my better judgment and before the meeting became contentious, I acquiesced." Sackett said. "I picked what I thought was the lesser evil. Better to let a kid on the team I didn't want than endure armchair decision-making from my superiors."

Martin was added back to the team and, perhaps out of guilt or on orders of a superior, named one of Seaholm's captains. This was the alpha moment of a disastrous season, and it wouldn't be the only time Sackett and Rosenthal sparred. Seaholm limped through 1987 with a 10-11 record. In most games they stayed close, but absorbed some ugly losses, too. They were smoked by Southfield Lathrup, 12-2. Kimball clobbered them, 12-5, in Game One of a doubleheader, although the Maples came back to win Game Two, 9-7. The highlight of the season was Martin's two-run triple to tie the West Bloomfield game with two outs in Seaholm's last at-bat, before he scored the winning run a few pitches later. The only other conference wins came over Southfield, Andover and Ferndale. Seaholm finished 5-11 in the SMA.

But the apex was Carroll's implosion in Seaholm's last home game of the season. Troy, who had defeated Seaholm the week prior, 6-4, were putting the screws down on the Maples when the hinges blew off.

The incident had been triggered by an innocuous pitching change. In the top of the sixth inning, Carroll disagreed loudly with Sackett's decision to swap pitchers while standing on the mound with his coach. After Carroll coughed up a passed ball allowing runners to move up, Sackett tossed at his critic a predictable blast from the dugout. Sackett thought, *"You can dish it out, Mike. If you want to second-guess my decisions, you better be able to take it, too."*

When the inning ended, Carroll and Sackett were already arguing by the time the rest of the team returned to the dugout. Soon thereafter, Sackett heard enough and replaced Carroll with Martin. Sackett thought, *"I didn't get this far by losing arguments with 16-year-olds."*

Carroll fired back with an ultimatum: "If I'm not in the field for the next inning, I quit." It was the fuse to light the powderkeg on the rest of the season.

"Coach Sackett called my bluff," Carroll said. "I deserved what I got."

The next day, just hours after Sackett asked himself how much worse it could get, he found out when Rosenthal called him into his office. Because Fraser and other parents reported the incident, Rosenthal was already aware of what happened when he called Sackett into his office. He asked his coach to recite the entire incident to him anyway.

It made Sackett feel like a dancing bear, and one thought dominated: *"This shit would have never happened under Mugsy."*

The Maples' interim athletic director and a former assistant Seaholm football coach prior to Rosenthal, Mugsy McInnis routinely grounded Seaholm's helicoptering parents. Rosenthal, by comparison, got a full statement from all involved before determining who was right and wrong. When Sackett was hired at Seaholm, an incident like Carroll's outburst would have forced his parents to drag their son back by his ear to apologize. Now parents and administrators forced Sackett to justify his decisions no matter what children behaving badly had done.

After Sackett finished making his statement, Rosenthal asked bluntly, "Would it have been such a bad thing to allow Mike to finish the game?"

While Sackett felt like asking, *"Do you realize the coach runs the team and not the kids?"* he also realized he was dealing with a superior who questioned his decision-making before the season started. He spoke to the middle ground Rosenthal was seeking before returning to his classroom, but after being questioned for the second time in as many days, he began questioning himself, too.

"Have the kids changed this much? Am I better off calling it a career? Have I stayed too long?"

It was not the first time he'd asked such questions. He had considered retiring after the 7-14 season of 1986, but his son, Mark, a 1983 graduate of Seaholm, talked him out of it. What ultimately brought Sackett back was a 182-81 (.692) record from 1975-86, winning over 20 games three different seasons. Sackett believed his Maples owned too much talent for something like 1986 to happen again. But from the start, this team sagged like a tree weighed down by heavy snow. It would eventually bend backwards further and further until it could bend no more. Carroll's searing meltdown had been the 'snap!' moment.

There was nothing to do but clean it up as best he could and move on. Already popular among Seaholm's well-to-do students in the hallways, Carroll was a rockstar after telling off his coach. While his former teammates lumbered through the final practices of the season, he hammered Sackett in every comment he made about the incident.

"I look back on it today and don't blame Coach Sackett for refusing to lose that argument," Carroll said. "He was the coach, I was the player and I was wrong. He wasn't going to be walked on by a 16-year-old hothead. But back then I killed him for it."

The last game of the year was at SMA rival Berkley and a pre-district qualifying game for the state tournament game, too. Moments before the team was scheduled to leave for the game, more drama unfolded in the parking lot. With players watching from inside the idling bus, Todd Glandt told Sackett he wouldn't play, sheepishly saying he turned his ankle in gym class earlier that day. A budding mutiny was afoot, and while Sackett didn't want to play the last game of the season without a substitute, he'd also learned his lesson from days earlier. Standing in his uniform with his clipboard and scorebook, the coach answered Glandt in calm, measured tones.

"That's fine, Todd. Before you make this decision final, I want you to know if you don't get on this bus, you'll never wear a Seaholm jersey for me again. In case you're wondering, that includes your senior year," Sackett said. He had hardly flexed a facial muscle while delivering the response. After an uncomfortable, pregnant pause between both of them, Sackett asked: "What do you want to do?"

An eerie silence followed. Neither coach or player shifted their weight or looked away. Instead, they stood eye to eye and toe to toe while most of the team watched from the bus.

Finally, Glandt blinked.

"Okay coach, I'll go."

Now feeling a bit taller, Sackett said with a stoneface, "Good. Get on the bus."

That was the only drama of the day. Berkley shut out the Maples, who were no-hit until Glandt singled in the sixth inning. In the days to follow, Sackett collected uniforms with no fanfare. There was no award ceremony, either, just a sleepy team dinner at Pasquale's in Royal Oak. The lynchpin of the stormy season, Martin led Seaholm in batting average (.311), triples and runs scored. If there was a last laugh during this terrible season, it belonged to him. He graduated a few weeks later. When final examinations were complete, Sackett cleaned out his desk and left, too.

Some needed soul-searching took place that summer. Sackett again evaluated his desire to coach. Determined not be forced out or asked to resign, his choices were clear: adjust his methods or hang up his cleats.

Carroll couldn't return to Seaholm's teams by just walking back through the door for his senior year —Sackett would never allow it — and after torching Fraser, he assumed there was no chance of playing football, either. His blow-up had painted him in a corner with just two options: call Sackett and apologize — and risk the embarrassment of an apology falling on deaf ears — or accept the arrangement his parents offered and attend Detroit Country Day. A well-to-do private school just a mile and half from Seaholm, the Yellowjackets had recently landed Chris Webber, an already nationally-known 14-year-old basketball prodigy that put Country Day on the national recruiting map. A few years later Shane Battier, Glandt's half-brother, would skip Seaholm for Country Day and follow Webber as a high school All-American.

Country Day had reached four Class C titles games, winning three baseball titles. Carroll would have a place to play and a chance to win a championship. June passed into July, which turned into August. Carroll took the entrance examination, passed and enrolled.

It was Aug. 25, four days from the first day of school at Country Day. Sackett wondered if his days as Seaholm's baseball coach were numbered. Carroll figured his days as a Maple were over.

CHAPTER TWO:

THE PHONE CALL

AS A RULE, COACHES DON'T APOLOGIZE AFTER BEING TOLD TO "go fuck themselves," and 17-year-old kids don't admit they're wrong after they've embarrassed themselves in front of their friends. But summer created some much-needed space between Don Sackett and Mike Carroll, headstrong combatants a couple months earlier.

In retrospect, their conflict was more superficial than real, male bravado and wounded pride more than genuine dislike for one another, and they both knew it. The question was, would either one admit it to the other? The answer came in the late morning hours Aug. 27, 1987. The phone rang at Bob Carroll's home on Hamilton in Birmingham and Don Sackett was on the other end of the call.

"Bob, this is Don Sackett. Is Mike available?" An uneasy few seconds followed and Sackett wondered if he might get blasted, making the olive branch he sought to offer a moot point. Carroll's parents, Bob and Susan, were divorced and Mike split time between their two separate homes.

"Hello, Coach. Is there something I can do for you?"

Sackett had to lay it on the line: "Bob, I'd like to talk to Mike about what happened last spring. It's been on my mind the entire summer. The truth is I like Mike, he's a good kid and I often think about what happened between us on that day. I want to talk to him to see if we can't repair things between us."

Don Sackett wasn't innocent, but his words were exactly what Bob Carroll wanted to hear. He knew Mike was wrong to have acted the way he did, and regardless of who was right or wrong, Sackett was the one in charge. His son should have respected that. *"This is a chance for Mike to climb out of the hole he dug for himself,"* Bob Carroll thought. If Mike didn't put his foot in his mouth again, it might save him thousands in tuition, too. This was a last chance for a couple of stubborn mules, one old and one young.

"Mike, you have a phone call. Come out here to the kitchen and take it," Bob Carroll said, while thinking, *"Mike, you better be on top of things during this call, this might be your last chance."*

Sackett allowed himself a brief exhale. There was still a chance to repair what they had broken between them, but he also knew this was far from fixed.

Over the summer, Mike admitted the truth to himself: he liked playing for Sackett. He loved the coach's quick wit, as direct as any coach he'd ever played for, and it was funny as hell when he'd zing a teammate or two. And like all the other Maples, he loved it when Sackett made fun of Clouser. Whether Sackett meant it or not didn't matter. Kimball owned the mental edge over Seaholm, and while the Maples respected them on the field, but there wasn't anyone at Seaholm who liked anything about Kimball.

But more than anything else, Carroll knew he was the guilty party for the dugout explosion. He'd allowed cockiness and pride to wreck himself. Yeah, maybe Sackett had baited him that day, but he deserved it. When Sackett said he was out of the game, Bob had told his son he should have taken the decision in stride and been a better teammate.

An unspoken silence permeated Carroll's house all summer. His behavior had created a consequence he had to live with, so to speak. There had been no looking back until the phone rang that morning.

Mike took the receiver from his father: "Hello?"

"Mike, it's Don Sackett. Do you have a minute?"

Over the next 30 minutes, a conversation transpired that would change the life of each of them. Each offered the other an apology for the ugly incident in the dugout. They admitted they had felt badly about the aftermath, too, a blow-up that spiraled out of control quickly because neither one of them had ever considered such a blow-up plausible.

With apologies out of the way, they glided easily into their old act. Mike told his coach about the summer team he played on and recalled some of the stories baseball lends itself Don told Mike of his summer spent with his family. In addition to the the Scrub-A-Dub car washes he owned with his brother-in-laws, he was also planning to purchase a yogurt shop — a franchise of the "I Can't Believe It's Yogurt" brand — in Bloomfield Hills. If it became a lucrative venture, it would be a healthy boost to a teacher's income for sure. Last, he shared the exploits of his son, Mark, who had followed in his father's footsteps as a Spartan baseball player and was scheduled to graduate from Michigan State in 1988 and would be coming back to Seaholm as an assistant coach.

Finally, he shared he was beginning to prepare for his retirement. His daughter, Shelly, was scheduled to graduate from Seaholm in 1990, a perfect time for him to exit, too. That statement resonated with Carroll. The incident in the dugout and quitting the team had put his coach in a tough spot with the school's administration for the second time that season. Of all the thoughts that went through Mike Carroll's mind during the phone call, one prevailed: *"Coach Sackett can't go out like this."*

Mike Carroll was seeing things differently, a stark difference from the last time they spoke three months earlier. Now they looked forward to seeing each other, and Don encouraged Mike to get into his senior math class.

Mike hung up the phone, turned to his father and said, "Dad, I want to go back to Seaholm." Bob Carroll could only smile because his son finally had displayed the maturity needed to fix the mess he had made for himself. He said to Mike, "Good. Seaholm is where you belong."

From in the recliner in the front room of his house on Arden Lane in Birmingham, Sackett eased back and exhaled. The new approach had worked for the old coach — the phone call was an unqualified success — and he could now see what some had tried to gently pass on for more than a few years. Rosenthal was incorrect in his assertion that Sackett should have allowed Carroll to stay in the game, but there was a modicum of truth that patience and understanding, in the right place, goes further.

"I was getting close to the end of my career, so I was inclined to just let the situation lie but because we had that big dust-up when he quit, I felt responsible for him wanting to go to Country Day," Sackett would say 30 years later.

The morning sun was now pouring through the windows of the Carroll home, an unintentional metaphor that Mike was in from the cold. Since he was old enough to remember, he wanted to be part of the Maples' rivalries with Groves and Kimball. Country Day was an outstanding a school as anyone could imagine but it was a second choice and an awkward end to high school.

Country Day had lost their new catcher, but the first seed of a miracle had been planted: Mike Carroll would remain a Maple.

CHAPTER THREE:

DON SACKETT

Head coach, Birmingham Seaholm, 1964-1990

IF IT'S TRUE THAT DON SACKETT'S SQUARE-JAWED, OLD-SCHOOL
principles didn't always mesh with the team he'd assembled in 1988,
it's fair to say his imperfect methodology was a perfect elixir to one of
Michigan's most improbable state title runs.

Unlikely would best describe the journey from Beaumont, Missouri
to Birmingham, Michigan. It included a handful of stops in minor league
baseball's sandlots and swamplands, a four-year tour in the Air Force and
four more years at Michigan State. He didn't immerse himself in the culture of high school baseball like his longtime adversary, Frank Clouser
but he remains the memorable icon among the players who went
through the program during his 27-year tenure as coach at Seaholm.
Among former Maples, Sackett's one-liners are told and retold often.

Sackett graduated from Beaumont High School in 1950. The
school is closed today, a casualty of three decades of declining student
performance and poor administrative leadership. Schools can't fix all
of the problems of the communities they serve no matter how much
we wish they could. Sometimes, it's better to close and start over somewhere else. It wasn't always that way in Beaumont, when the school
was bursting at the seams with over 4,000 students post-World War II.

The school produced a half-dozen future major league players and
one future Hall of Fame manager, Earl Weaver. Sackett and Weaver
were teammates in 1949. Weaver was a shortstop while Sackett pitched
on the rare occasions he got to play.

"I think I pitched in two games as a senior; it was tough to get on the field," Sackett said.

After signing with the St. Louis Cardinals out of high school, Weaver bounced around the minor leagues before being traded to Baltimore, where he led the Baltimore Orioles to six pennants and three World Series titles. Sackett followed a similar path, signing a minor league contract with the Cleveland Indians in January of 1951.

"I went to spring training in Daytona Beach with the team like a walk-on in college football or basketball," Sackett said. "I didn't expect to last long — they had Bob Feller, Bob Lemon, Early Wynn and Larry Doby — but I did well enough that they sent me to a farm team in Green Bay, Wisconsin."

After Green Bay, he went to Alabama to play for the Enterprise Boll Weevils of the Class D Alabama-Florida League. He started 12 of the 18 games he appeared in, going 5-6 with a WHIP of 1.541, so a call-up to the big club wasn't imminent. Still, he hit .270 with three doubles, a triple and a home run in 63 at-bats.

"I did pretty well but I was bouncing around, filling spots here and there," Sackett said. "One night in Panama City, Florida, I was playing right field, the lights weren't too good and there are frogs jumping all around me. I prayed they didn't hit the ball to me."

With a career in professional baseball unlikely — "I was up against too many professional ball players" — Sackett turned down a promotion in 1952 to Class C ball in the swamp-laden Florida State League to join the Air Force.

Over the next four years he bounced between stations and airfields in California, Illinois, Mississippi and Kansas. When his tour ended, he traded Air Force blue for Michigan State green. He could afford MSU with money made and saved in the Air Force, serving as a Resident Advisor in MSU's Bailey Hall and a small stipend to play baseball. He also worked weekends on the farm on two uncles living 50 miles south of East Lansing.

"It was a pretty nice life. Too bad I had to study once in a while," Sackett said.

It was while playing baseball for MSU he earned his "Old Man" nickname, thanks to Bill Schudlich, a former Detroit Tigers scout now working for the Cleveland Indians. Because he was the oldest player on the MSU team, Schudlich's nickname for Sackett stuck, to no one's surprise.

"We had Ron Perranoski and Rick Radatz from Berkley High School, and we should have won a couple Big Ten titles," Sackett said. "All we had to do was beat Minnesota to win the 1958 Big Ten title. Radatz was pitching and he was standing on third base when someone hit a fly ball. For some reason, he didn't tag up. We would have won, 2-1, but Minnesota ended up winning the championship. He's probably the reason why they invented the designated hitter."

Sackett was Michigan State's Opening Day pitcher in 1959, earning a 7-2 win at Purdue. He pitched a good game at Michigan despite losing 2-1 and getting a base hit. But his command of the strike zone waned and his senior year ended on the bench.

"I know what I was doing wrong now, but back then you didn't get a lot of instruction," Sackett said. "You either threw strikes and pitched or you didn't throw strikes and found yourself on the bench."

This blunt-force, trauma-to-the-head communication would shape Sackett's decision-making and delivery in his coaching career. With his playing days finished, Sackett landed a student-teaching gig to finish his degree in the fall of 1960. Nearly 30 and in need of a full-time job, Christmas arrived early when a math teacher at Seaholm resigned to move to California with her husband. In the span of a 30-second phone call, the understudy was a full-time teacher.

He didn't coach that following spring, but landed an unpaid assistant's position under coach Sam Tassio the following year. In 1963, Tassio gave Sackett $50 for his efforts.

"That was big money because there was no freshman or junior varsity back then," Sackett said. "It didn't seem like a big deal but that was my foot in the door."

A year later, the importance of that hire would be crystalized when Tassio retired to become a park ranger in Wyoming. In need of a new coach, Dave Godschalk would have logically been next in line for the job, but he had taken the open position at Birmingham Groves a year earlier. With his college and pro baseball experience, and two years under his belt as a Seaholm assistant, the "Old Man" was an instant solution to an immediate problem. With a short walk down the hall, Seaholm's principal conducted the shortest coaching interview in the history of high school sports.

"He walked into my room and said, 'We need a new baseball coach — will you take this off my hands?'" Sackett said. "It took all of four seconds. We were in the middle of the first year of the SMA, and I was immediately coaching in a powerhouse league. Hazel Park was the toughest team in the league. Ferndale was good, too. We beat Kimball almost every time because Clouser wasn't there yet."

Sackett's early teams enjoyed some phenomenal success. At Berkley for a night game that initial season, Seaholm's Mike Fremuth struck out 19 of 21 hitters that evening. In those days, the baseball coach at many schools was also the football coach, some using baseball as a training program. Almost every week, Sackett was coaching against at least one Hall of Fame legend.

"Paul Temerian, and later Herb Deromedi, coached baseball at Kimball. Al Fracassa was the coach at Brother Rice. For a lot of years, John Herrington coached the team at Farmington Hills Harrison. They were great football coaches, but we were beating those schools on a regular basis," Sackett said. "I had some great teams in the 1960s and we won a couple of league championships. It was a big deal because there was no state tournament."

That would change in 1971. With the help of Clouser, the MHSAA began sponsoring a state tournament and the schools on Sackett's annual schedule quickly became some of the most accomplished programs in Michigan. Hazel Park went to the finals in 1974 and 1976 under Chuck Mikulas. Clarkston and West Bloomfield won titles in 1976 and 1983 respectively. Birmingham Brother Rice emerged, making their first finals appearance in 1986. Kimball, which went to four Class A title games from 1971-80, narrowly missed other finals appearances with a handful of losses in the regional finals.

Sackett's teams were successful in the SMA, but that same consistency eluded the Maples in the state tournament. But more than the great teams, coaches and athletes Seaholm faced, one event threatened to derail Sackett's association with Seaholm baseball.

The death of Scott Dunkel would make Sackett consider quitting.

April 23, 1973 was an evening a number of Seaholm players went to an impromptu spring break party in Birmingham. When the party broke up, some players drove home in a car while Dunkel decided to walk. His teammates in the car playfully engaged their teammate in a game of chicken, and as is the case with most teenagers, no one was thinking about the "what if" consequences. When Dunkel and the car went in the same direction at the point they each had to dodge each other, a tragedy of immense proportions had been created in a few short seconds by an unintended accident.

Sackett, with no knowledge of the party, was devastated along with the rest of Birmingham. The team's first game to follow was against Brother Rice, and a rival became a friend.

"Fracassa put his arm around my shoulder before the game and said, 'I know it's tough, but these kids are at their lowest moment and they need you more than ever,'" Sackett said, as Fracassa continued, "You didn't have anything to do with this, but if you leave now, what does that tell them? Trust me, this will pass.'"

"That's the kind of guy Fracassa was," Sackett said.

Fracassa was right. Sackett stayed and Seaholm continued to win, despite the frustration of the state tournament.

The 1981 Maples might have been Sackett's most talented team, featuring Division I talents C.J. Beschke (Michigan), Rick Ziegler (Eastern Michigan), Dave Harris (Ball Starte) and Greg Lotzar (Central Michigan). After Kimball made it to the state final the year before, Seaholm easily won the SMA and eliminated the Knights in that year's district semifinal. But against Bloomfield Hills Andover, which saved their best pitcher for Seaholm, the Maples lost, 3-2.

"That loss might be my biggest regret because it was my best team, better than the 1988 and 1989 teams," Sackett said.

By the mid-1980s, the game, the student-athlete and the responsibilities of the coach changed. Suffering some indignities in the 1987 season that other coaches might have walked away from, Sackett instead looked in the mirror. He changed some of his acerbic ways and while the changes might have seemed slight, it opened the door for an epic moment in Birmingham's history. True to his 27 years on Seaholm's bench, Sackett looks back on his career with appreciation for what was and wasn't.

"A lot of great coaches don't win at all, and I didn't win with my best teams," Sackett says, "but if you coach long enough, you're bound to win sometime. And we did."

CHAPTER FOUR:

A WITCH'S BREW

HIS SENIOR YEAR WAS SAVED BUT MIKE CARROLL WASN'T ON

the sidelines with his teammates when Seaholm opened the 1987 football season against Bloomfield Hills Lahser.

In Michigan, the first football game is the unofficial start of the school year. Carroll, who could have easily been one of Seaholm's defensive backs, could only watch as Seaholm struggled in a disappointing 14-12 loss. Back then, the MHSAA playoffs afforded just 32 teams in each of the four classes for the playoffs; the loss all but eliminated the Maples from playoff contention in the first week of the season.

The next week, things didn't improve much. The Maples lost the league opener to Berkley, traditionally an SMA doormat, 14-10. Looking up at the rest of the SMA, Fraser's squad recovered by winning three straight, including thumping Kimball on homecoming, 27-6. In that game, Siefken threw a 31-yard touchdown to Matt Newton, while Kevin Billington ran roughshod for 144 yards and a touchdown. Losses to Troy and Ferndale ruined any chance of winning the SMA, and the Maples entered the final week of the season at 4-4. The final game of the season was Birmingham Groves in the 80,000-seat Pontiac Silverdome, a date they shared with Royal Oak's two public high schools. Seaholm chopped down the Falcons, 13-8; Dondero overwhelmed Kimball, 27-7.

Meanwhile, a minor miracle occurred for Seaholm's boys' soccer team, albeit slightly less captivating than the one to follow in the spring. After finishing far behind champion Troy and runner-up Kimball in the SMA, the Maples entered the state tournament with little expectation. Inexplicably, Seaholm won the district, with the help of Steve Sheckell, their 6-foot-4 goaltender.

"I was a very average player, and our team was very average, but winning our district my senior year was a shocking outcome," Sheckell said. "Troy was in our league – they beat us twice – but they weren't in our district, and we beat Andover in the final, which was a bit of a miracle, too." Fall turning into winter is one of the most exciting times of the prep calendar. Michigan has always played a nine-game schedule and since 1975, the state football finals have been married with the Thanksgiving Day weekend, following the Detroit Lions' traditional holiday home game. Until 2007, the state's football playoffs ran alongside the girls' basketball tournament. An ill-conceived but ultimately successful lawsuit forced Michigan to move the girls' basketball season in the traditional winter season and transfer volleyball to the fall.

An important aside here: It's been over a decade since the change, and participation numbers in both sports have slumped, creating a perplexing legacy for this federal court order that superceded the MHSAA's decision to exhaust the appeal process. Girls basketball participation has fallen 18 percent, while volleyball has fallen nearly 10 percent. Some of the decline has to do with Michigan's overall decline in population and high school enrollment, but not everyone in Michigan agrees this decision falls in line with what Title IX has done to help advance girls playing sports.[1]

In football, the last game of the regular season normally was against your traditional rival, and basketball season opened with that same rival. In Birmingham, the boys' basketball season started with Groves and the Maples were optimistic their teams would be formidable.

Ferndale, coached by Gary Sophia and led by Dwayne Stephens, were the favorites to win the SMA. In Southfield, coach Greg Swifka

---

1   Hugh Bernreuter, "Who has benefited from seismic change to Michigan high school sports seasons," *MLive Media Group*, August 29, 2018. Retrieved from http://mlive.com

was gone, removed two years earlier when a physical altercation with a student ended his tenure. The Blue Jays still had over 100 athletes try out for the team, so they were, at a minimum, able and athletic. Troy's team would also be formidable. Not nearly as talented as a Southfield or Ferndale in a raw context, the Colts won with fundamentally-strong defensive sets and just enough offense to hang around and wear you down.

Seaholm, featuring Dave Marcinkowski as a bruising post presence and Steve Sheckell as an outside shooting threat, figured to be best among the rest of the SMA teams. Statewide, the news surrounding the opening the basketball season was the Michigan High School Athletic Association's approval of a three-point line. At just 19-feet-9, shooters from all over the state were poised to take aim.

On Friday, Jan. 9, 1988, the Maples hosted Berkley and Sheckell went off, dropping 52 on the Bears in leading Seaholm to a 109-69 win. He made a jaw-dropping 11 3-point shots and scored 19 the old-fashioned way, too.

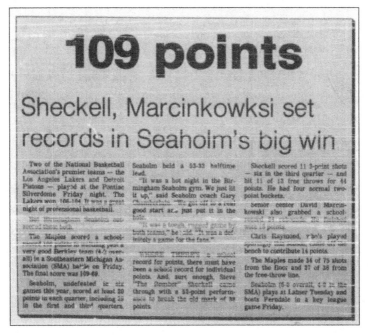

Seaholm's 109-69 win over Berkley, headlined by Steve Sheckell's 52-point effort, made big headlines across metro Detroit, including this edition of the *Observer & Eccentric*.

"I can't remember where we were at that night, but I remember being in the gym after we heard about him scoring 50," Kimball's Steve Kinkade said. "Berkley was notoriously tough defensively, so for them to give up over 100 and let someone go for 50 got everyone's attention."

With Sheckell on the wing and Marcinkowski underneath, Seaholm roared past Andover, Berkley, Hazel Park, Kimball and Southfield. The Maples would battle for the league title, falling short by two games, tying for second with Troy at 11-3 in the SMA and 17-3 overall. In the district playoffs, Seaholm won their first two games. On the other side of the bracket, Brother Rice easily outpaced Groves, 71-46, to set up a district championship between Seaholm and Brother Rice for the fourth time in five years and the 11th time overall in state tournament play.

Brother Rice had eliminated the Maples in eight of the previous 10 meetings. The Warriors had built themselves into a premier program by winning 14 district titles, playing in two state finals (1974, 1977) and reaching four semifinals. Seaholm, by comparison, had won just two district titles in 25 years.

Hopes were high that Friday night because this was the best team Seaholm offered in the past several years. Meeting at West Bloomfield High School that evening, referee Joe Marcinkowski sought to diffuse any animosity building between the two schools.

"I knew this was a big moment in Birmingham, two local schools meeting in a final, and there was a definite tension in the air that night," Marcinkowski said. "I happened to have the same name as one of the captains at Seaholm, so I decided to have a little fun with it. We get the captains from Rice and Seaholm together at midcourt and I look at Dave Marcinkowski and say, 'How's Uncle Henry doing?' Rice's captains have this weird look on their faces. After a few seconds go by, and I admit we aren't related, that we never met and it was all a gag born strictly of circumstance. They all burst out laughing and it broke the rigid posturing."

Seaholm's state tournament frustrations in basketball were just as pronounced as they were in baseball. At 19-3, the 1987-88 Maples fielded one of their best teams in over a decade, and they still couldn't escape neighboring Birmingham Brother Rice in the district final, as reported by the *Observer & Eccentric*.

Marcinkowski was in foul trouble most of the night while Brother Rice's stout defense handcuffed Sheckell. Historically, Catholic League schools play a much more physical brand of basketball than their suburban counterparts, and it showed on this night. The Warriors eliminated Seaholm once again, 62-52.

Sheckell was named the *Observer & Eccentric's* Player of the Year after leading the SMA with 26.6 points per game. He made the *Daily Tribune's* first team and earned First Team All-Suburban honors from the *Detroit Free Press*, too. He'd made a name for himself by shooting a remarkable 55.3 percent (88 of 159) from behind the arch — while making 82% of his free throws. His proficiency, plus Seaholm's 19-4 overall record, made Sheckell was a necessary inclusion on almost every publication's all-state team at some level, including Honorable

Mention on the Free Press' All-State team. He shared mentions with players such as Chris Webber and Steve Avery.

Ferndale's Dwayne Stephens, the best player in the SMA, was named to the *Detroit Free Press* All-State Third Team. Detroit Cooley won the Class A basketball title, the second of three-straight titles for coach Ben Kelso's Cardinals, and part of a bigger Detroit domination. A Detroit Public School League school won every Class A title from 1987-1994.

With basketball finished, the focus at Seaholm turned to spring sports. There would be no Dave Martin controversy. Sackett admitted to himself over the summer some of his methods required some change, but remained adamant to himself and those close to him that in a rush to appease his athletic director and principal, he'd too easily dismissed an important coaching tenet: if it's your team, pick the team you want. If the school administration wants a 'Yes' man, they can make a change but as long as he's coach, he'll keep his dignity in place and pick the team. With most of his team was already in place, Sackett emerged as a perfect leader for the most unlikely of tournament contenders. Carroll would catch. Siefken was Seaholm's No. 1 pitcher. Matt Newton, a football star and the team's cocky firebrand, would play third. Sheckell was likely the state's tallest second baseman. Rob Kaye manned shortstop and Glandt handled first base. The outfield, from left to right, would be manned by Jeff Millius, Bret Russell and Cameron Mueller. The only question was how this group would match up with Kimball. The Knights won the SMA in 1987 and were favorites in 1988, and in Sackett's mind, were due for another signature run through districts and regionals. But there were some cracks in Kimball's armor. Clouser's pitching staff didn't boast a lights-out fireballer that trademarked his program from the late 1960s through the mid-1980s. Among the local newspapers and Detroit's two metro dailies, high school baseball previews are assembled with calls to a handful of established, successful coaches. Clouser likely took a call every year, while the suburban dailies preview every school and each program gets a few kids mentioned. To no one's surprise, when the previews came out, almost every publication picked Kimball to win the SMA. For the last 20 years, Kimball had been the team to beat not just in the SMA, but in Oakland County. No one foresaw the changes within a handful of teams evolving over the next three months that would turn the state tournament on its ear.

CHAPTER FIVE:

STEVE SHECKELL

Class of 1988, Birmingham Seaholm

JUST LIKE HE WAS IN HIGH SCHOOL, STEVE SHECKELL REMAINS

smart and talented, methodical and introspective. With these qualities, it's no surprise Sheckell's life has turned out like most thought it would. Since 2004, he's been successful with the firm Ernst & Young, first as an audit partner, then as a team leader in Michigan and Ohio and for the last two years, as a managing partner in the company's Detroit office.

He's dedicated his life's work to crunching facts, figures and numbers for a living, but Sheckell is still remembered among the friends he grew up with for just one number.

52.

In the spring of 1987, the National Federation of High Schools (NFHS) made the 3-point line mandatory. Michigan had been one of the states experimenting with the line in prior seasons. Now the line was official and public awareness sped up considerably Jan. 9, 1988, the Saturday morning after Sheckell, Marcinkowski and Seaholm set a handful of state and school records in beating Berkley, 109-69. Seaholm's 109 points was a record for a school that opened in 1904, and Sheckell knocked down 11 3's — including six in the third quarter — to smash the previous Seaholm record of 38 for points in a game by a player.

It immediately set the MHSAA record for 3's in a game, a record Sheckell shared for two years with Brian Pumford from Newaygo, who also hit 11 in a game that season. Only seven players in MHSAA history have since eclipsed Sheckell's 11 3's that night.

Sheckell also scored 19 the old-fashioned way with four 2-point field goals and 11 free throws. Meanwhile, Marcinkowski pulled down 34 rebounds, setting the Seaholm record and tying him for ninth all-time in state history with three other players, notably Detroit Pershing's Spencer Haywood, the first player to ever go directly from high school to the NBA.

All of it grabbed the attention of anyone who kept a trained high on Michigan's prep sports scene. The *Detroit Free Press* inserted a special game box on the prep page the next day with a small write-up on a suburban game that ordinarily would get two lines of agate-sized font. Sheckell's name was immediately thrust into the mind of every college coach in the state, even if for just a brief moment.

The *Detroit Free Press* inserted a special text box on the morning after Steve Sheckell scored 52 points against Berkley, then made him their high school Athlete of the Week a few days later.

"I remember hearing about that game because I recruited the SMA quite a bit," said Ben Braun, who was then in his second full season coaching at Eastern Michigan. "If you scored 50 points in a Class A game in southeastern Michigan back then, it got a lot of attention."

There's a lot that goes into getting offered an athletic scholarship to play college basketball, even more for Division I basketball, and finally, major college basketball. First, it's not an exact science; coaches don't always get it right. Second, some coaches are fearful of the optics of offering a player no one else is recruiting instead of trusting their own evaluation of that player's ability to succeed or fail within their program.

"I asked three questions when I recruited a player," Braun said. "Would I want to play against this player? If the answer was no, I asked myself if this player will succeed in our system? If that answer was yes, did I have a spot on my team for this player? This is what makes recruiting difficult for the player and coach."

Sheckell landed at Division III Albion College. He admits the experience was startling.

"I got looked at by a small handful of Division III schools and had a good career at Albion, but not as good as I thought it would be when I got there," Sheckell said. "I had to improve a lot of my game, like playing defense and rebounding. It was a big adjustment."

His natural talent carried him past inferior competition at Seaholm, but his deficiencies threatened his success at Albion. In addition to working on footwork and form that accompanies jump-shooting, or dribble-drive skills when attacking the rim, Sheckell had to become a star in weight room and conditioning drills. Fatigue is the great thief of skill and ability. You need a strong upper body to absorb contact from defenders. Strong legs add lift to your shot. He needed to get better at coming off screens and creating space for himself as a shooter. He learned how to defend because no coach needs a scorer who's a defensive liability.

A high school star unaware of the work required to succeed when he arrived at Albion College, Steve Sheckell's decision to address his deficiencies as a player turned him into one of the greatest performers in the school's long history. *(Albion College)*

This is the world jump shooters live within, and as Sheckell immersed himself in this work, he became a star in one of the toughest Division III leagues in the country. He hasn't played a game for the Britons in over 25 years, but the first name you see is Sheckell's on the Albion basketball records page. Most points in a single game? That's Sheckell, with 48 in 1992 against Olivet College. Most 3's made in a single game? That's 10, also by Steve Sheckell, also against Olivet.

He holds school records for most 3's attempted in a game, most free throws attempted and made in a single game, and best 3-point percentage in a single game, going 7 for 8 against Spring Arbor and Olivet. His 531 points in the 1991-92 season is good for third-best in a single season. His 1,247 career points places him sixth all-time in Albion history. Marcinkowski is ninth with 1,215 points.

"I wound up having a good junior year and great senior year, but we were playing in a league with Hope and Calvin, two of the top 10 teams in the country," Sheckell said. "Calvin went 31-1 and won the national championship, and Hope was ranked in the top 10 at 26-4. They have a really famous rivalry and attract outstanding players."

Today, Sheckell lives in Bloomfield Hills. He's married with three kids, including oldest son Drew, who followed his footsteps into college basketball at Kalamazoo College. He draws on two experiences — Miracle Maples and overcoming his deficiencies at Albion — most often in his professional life.

"I'm glad I did all of it, because sports taught me a life's worth of lessons on teamwork and integrity, of hard work and leadership," Sheckell said. "I use a lot of things I learned in sports at work, in the form of analogies that can be applied in the office."

What specifically did the Miracle Maples experience teach?

"You can't go half speed; you have to keep competing. When we got beat by Kimball in that doubleheader — this is one of those sports analogies I use at work all the time — we lost as a team," Sheckell said. "We couldn't blame each other. We had to figure how to make it better going forward. You pull yourself off the ground and go try again and compete, and that's what we did."

"We lacked the confidence we needed to beat Kimball but I think that loss was a blessing in disguise. Winning those two games against Lathrup and Rice the way we did in the state tournament gave us the confidence to keep winning. That's the turning point between winning and losing, in sports or in business or in life. Just like you've got to see the ball go through the hoop, you've got to win a game or two like that. And once you do, you believe it can and will happen every time."

CHAPTER SIX:

THE RIVAL

"FRANK CLOUSER'S AN ASSHOLE!"

Anyone who played baseball for Seaholm in the 1980s remembers this as Don Sackett's favorite phrase. Clouser, the head coach at Kimball since 1969, had made life miserable for Sackett and the Maples. Starting in 1971, Kimball grabbed the prep baseball scene in Oakland County by the throat. They appeared in the first three Class A championship games and won the SMA four straight years. Clouser's teams won 93 of 119 games in 1971-74, including a stretch of 20 straight wins in 1974, and 36 of 37 dating back to 1973, the only loss in the state final to Detroit Western. In 1974, Clouser was named *Associated Press'* Class A Coach of the Year, when Kimball went 26-2 but didn't make it to the state finals.

The characteristics of Clouser's Kimball teams was talented pitching, amazing defense and Clouser's affinity for bunting.

"I went to Novi High School, and Kimball was well-known as a powerhouse, a big school with great coaches and a lot of good athletes. We knew their story well," says Greg Porter, who coached Seaholm nine seasons over two different appointments, was the interim head coach at Oakland University and now coaches Royal Oak High School. "They were loaded with players who could pitch and play defense, so in most games they only needed one or two runs to win."

The Maples' frustration with Kimball was two-fold. They finished behind Kimball in the SMA chronically and worse, had never advanced past the district since the tournament's inception in 1971. The league and district was dominated by their Royal Oak rivals.

"That was coach Sackett's most hated team for sure, but they always beat us so that was part of it," Sheckell said. "Baseball is different than football or basketball in terms of rivalry — it's not the nature of the game — but I think when you have trouble beating someone and they have your number, it's logical who your rival is. For us, that was Kimball."

And regarding Sackett's comment about the Kimball coach, his audience comprised of testosterone-fueled teenagers weren't entirely fooled.

"There couldn't have two more separate people than Coach Sackett and Coach Clouser in the way they coached and the way they approached the game," Siefken said. "Sackett would have a couple signs for the day, and Clouser would have an entire set of strategies ready to put into the game."

Sackett didn't really hate Clouser. Like most county coaches, Sackett respected Kimball for being a fundamentally sound program while accomplishing an amazing feat: four appearances in the Class A title game in 10 years. The respect among coaches carried past the field, too. Clouser had played a key role in the formation of the the state's baseball coaches association and the MHSAA state tournament — it was modeled after Indiana's state tournament, his home state.

Don Sackett (L) and Frank Clouser chat along the third base line during Sackett's last visit to Kimball May 1, 1990. *Photo by Craig Gaffield (The Daily Tribune)*

What Sackett hated was losing to Clouser. He hated watching Kimball outpitch the competition, and how they bunted relentlessly to move runners up. How they pressured the opposition's defense to make plays. Most of all, he hated watching his teams make mistakes against Clouser's simple strategies.

"My senior year, I threw a great game against them and we still lost, 10-0," said Mark Sackett of a 1983 loss. "They bunted, and we kicked it around like Little Leaguers. They made no mistakes. It was miserable."

Sackett also hated that Kimball defeated some of his best teams, too. There was a real sense of satisfaction when players like Dave Harris, Greg Lotzar, Rick Ziegler and C.J. Beschke helped Seaholm wrest the SMA crown from Kimball in 1981. But successes like this were short-lived. Seaholm was 13-1 in the SMA, 20-2 overall and beat Kimball three times. They were ranked in the top 5 of every local and statewide poll. But in the district playoffs, Seaholm lost. Again.

The mental block that came from consistently losing to Kimball was something Sackett was determined to break. In making fun of Clouser, he was using the same strategy Herb Brooks, Team USA's hockey coach in 1980, used to demystify the legend of Soviet Union forward Boris Mikhailov in front of his team. The most accomplished Soviet Union player, Mikhailov bore an uncanny resemblance to Stan Hardy, and Brooks made fun of it constantly.

"Before I moved to Birmingham, I lived in Clawson, and I had a lot of friends who went to Kimball," said Siefken, the Maples' best pitcher and Seaholm's quarterback in 1986-87. "It was a rivalry that had been established by classes who came before us."

During the 1970s, a Kimball baseball game was a much bigger event than could ever be imagined today. By 1977, Brad Havens and Steve Manderfield both threw in the high 90s and formed a terrifying one-two combination for opponents.

"Havens could put the ball wherever he wanted, so you couldn't hit him," says Little, who played at Seaholm in 1974-78. "Manderfield could throw it down the middle, and you couldn't catch up to it. The next one would be at your head, and you couldn't get out of the way. Manderfield was in your kitchen the minute you stepped in the box."

Mark Sackett remembers Seaholm pulling off what was then considered one of the biggest wins in school history during the 1977 season. "I was 12 years old, Dad's team was hosting Kimball and I ran home from school to see the game," Sackett said. "I grabbed my mother's bike and raced up to school as fast as I could. Dad hadn't beaten Kimball in three or four years and Havens, who everyone thought would be a major leaguer, was pitching. It seemed like everyone I knew was at the game. In the bottom of the seventh, with two outs and two strikes, Scott Wilson singled home Jeff Maher and they walked Kimball off, 2-1. It was beyond huge."

Sackett jumped back on that bike and raced home in tears.

"I ran in the door screaming for my Mom. She sees me and literally starts screaming: 'What is wrong? Tell me what's wrong!'" Sackett said. "I'm so happy, I can barely get the words out of my mouth…"

'They won, Mom! – THEY WON! – They beat Kimball!'"

In May 1982, Clouser won his 300th game, a 12-0 win over Rochester Adams, and the *Detroit Free Press* sent Mick McCabe to write a profile. He discovered a staggering fact: in those 300 victories, 100 had been shutouts and 25 had been no-hitters or perfect games. That's one in every 12 Kimball wins ending as a no-hitter.

In most games, Clouser kept his foot on the throat of his opponents and he was despised for it.

"Clouser ran it up on all of us, and it pissed a lot of coaches off," Don Sackett said. "The coaches in the county respected his knowledge and the ability of his teams, but he wouldn't pull his starters and he didn't stop bunting. One year, before Michigan had a 10-run mercy rule, he beat us 19-0. I never forgave him for it."

Sackett was guilty of the same crime, too. Bookending the aforementioned 2-1 win over Kimball in 1977, Sackett beat Bloomfield Hills Lahser, 13-2, and slaughtered Berkley, 23-5, the game after.

Clouser admits his will to win was sometimes unpopular, sometimes within in his own building.

"I don't remember beating him 19-0, but if I lost 19-0, I'd probably be mad, too," Clouser said. "The one criticism my athletic director had was I was too competitive. Early in my career, I was not going to give up outs. I don't know if I would do those things again. I busted my butt to get the best out of our kids that I could. And I didn't like to lose."

In this context, Groves trailed a distant second to Kimball as a rival for the Maples.

"We were expected to beat Groves, but there wasn't anything we liked about Kimball, and I'm sure they felt the same way about us, too," Kauth said. "The games with Kimball were tougher, so they were bigger."

Compounding this angst for many schools was Kimball's powerful football program. The Knights won 183 of 245 football games (.759) from 1957-1983, taking 11 league titles and never suffering a losing record. Royal Oak Dondero, Kimball's archrival, went 170-83-6 during the same period. The two schools regularly played in front of 5,000-6,000 fans; when they played each other, it wasn't uncommon to draw between 8,000-10,000 fans.

Paul Temerian, a gruff, intense Armenian whose demand for discipline paired him perfectly with the game he loved and the school he coached on Friday nights.

"Paul Temerian terrified me," said former Royal Oak *Daily Tribune* sports editor Steve Stein. "Kimball was *the* red-letter game for almost every school it played back then because they were tough as nails."

Paul Temerian, shown here winning his 100th game at Ferndale in 1980, was the source of frustration for many opponents. With 10 league titles and a record of 131-39-1, his Kimball teams ruined seasons for multiple schools year after year. *(Metro Detroit's High School Football Rivalries/Daily Tribune)*

By 1981, the Kimball-Dondero game had outgrown Royal Oak. The two rivals were ranked No. 1 and No. 2 in the state — both were undefeated and league champions — when they played the "Battle Royal," the nickname given to the game by the Detroit News. The game had been moved from the traditional Friday night slot to Saturday afternoon because of security concerns about the anticipated crowd size. An estimated 10,000 fans watched Kimball win the game, 17-7, and carry Temerian off the field in celebration of Kimball's 21st-straight win dating back to 1979. The next year, the game was moved to the 80,000-seat Pontiac Silverdome, played as a doubleheader with Birmingham's Seaholm-Groves game. By combining the location for both games on the same night, the two games drew 12,000 fans."

"The 1986 Kimball game was one of those games you wish for as a kid — it was a Mud Bowl in the mud, rain and slop — but actually playing it wasn't a whole lot of fun," Siefken said. "Jim Sonnenburg ran the opening kickoff of the second half for a touchdown to beat us, 6-3. That one play cost us the game and it might have kept us out of the playoffs."

Kimball's success earned them plenty of jealousy. No matter how important another school's game was, the headlines in Saturday morning's paper often belonged to Kimball. Their game with Dondero was known statewide as one of the biggest rivalries in Michigan, often deciding a perfect season, a No. 1 ranking or a berth in the state playoffs. If some opposing coaches and athletic directors hated the constant attention diverted away from their own programs, Royal Oak's *Daily Tribune*, and Detroit's metro dailies, the *Detroit News* and *Free Press*, gobbled it up.

"Paul Temerian taught me to call the result of every game in to the papers, win or lose," Clouser said. "Instead of having to talk to a student manager or a parent, newspaper reporters liked to hear from you personally. When you win, and you're an open book, people want to know why you're winning, what your strategy is and the philosophy you use. And then, when reporters visited, we made our kids accessible. That helped us get a lot more attention than other schools."

But by the late 1980s, Kimball's football fortunes had fallen off a cliff. In Temerian's last five seasons, Kimball went 32-5 and won the SMA twice; George Hanoian took over in 1984 after Temerian retired and went 19-35. He posted just one winning record in six seasons after Kimball had rattled off 27 years without a losing record.

Seaholm, meanwhile, was surging. Under Chuck Skinner and later, Doug Fraser, the Maples won 136 games over the next 17 seasons, and defeated Kimball in 10 of those years after losing 10 of the preceding 11 before Skinner's arrival. Seaholm became annual contenders to win the SMA and later, the Oakland Activities Association (OAA) while Fraser, with his 76-31 record, became the winningest coach in Seaholm history. By the mid-1980s, Troy was an emerging powerhouse who made it to the Class A title game in 1985 and 1994. It was obvious Kimball had been passed in football by most of the SMA schools.

Chuck Skinner transferred from the gritty enclave of Hazel Park to the posh address of Birmingham Seaholm, but he continued to win, turning the Maples into annual contenders for the SMA championship and state playoff berths. *Photo by Gary Caskey (Hometown Life)*

"The Kimball game wasn't everything, but they were a rival, and trust me when I say I did not mind pounding them into the ground our senior year," Siefken said of trouncing Kimball, 27-7, on Seaholm's homecoming in 1987.

Meanwhile, Clouser's program hadn't seriously competed for a state title since losing a heartbreaker in the regional final in 1983 to eventual state champion West Bloomfield. This was the second seed planted in the Maples' miracle season. The Maples had never advanced past the district, but Don Sackett thought, *"Why not us? Why not now?"*

The pride that meant everything at Kimball was slipping away and Seaholm had nothing to lose. They were a gambler putting a fistful of house cash on the puncher minutes before everyone else realizes the odds have changed and the casino stops taking bets. This was precious currency to spur the Maples' title run.

Don Sackett was sitting on raw talent, its' potential just simmering beneath the visible surface. The question was could he harness it, and how would he do it before it was wasted? Again.

CHAPTER SEVEN:

FRANK CLOUSER

Head coach, Royal Oak Kimball, 1969-1995

IF HIS CAREER WAS SUMMED UP IN A SENTENCE ON THE GAME

show *Jeopardy*, the sentence might read like this: "This former Indiana farm boy is one of the godfathers of Michigan's high school baseball tournament."

Who is Frank Clouser?

Synonymous with baseball at Kimball for almost three decades, Clouser's legacy is his role in bringing a statewide tournament to high school baseball at a time when, except for basketball, the MHSAA sponsored no other championships.

He was hired at Kimball in 1968 and a year later, in either the late summer or early fall of 1969, Clouser and Bill Boyd, the baseball coach at Royal Oak Dondero, drove up to Cadillac, Michigan. They met with Cadillac's Ted Fewless and two other coaches. Within this group, Clouser started constructing the pillars of Michigan's current baseball tournament and the Michigan High School Baseball Coaches Association, which sponsors the East-West All-Star Game at Comerica Park and before that, Tiger Stadium.

"We had a baseball tournament before we had a football tournament because of Clouser," Don Sackett said, a nod to Michigan's many high schools where football remains the most popular sport. But football didn't have a tournament until 1975, four years after the baseball tournament was approved.

61

He grew up on a small farm in Colfax, Indiana, now less than 700 residents, the product of a simple life. Working on the farm and school came first. He stayed up late in the spring and summer listening to Red Barber's broadcasts of the Dodgers, first from Brooklyn and later Los Angeles, especially when Sandy Koufax pitched. At Colfax High School, he was a star in baseball and basketball.

"It would be easy to say Frank owned most of our school records because we were a small school, but Frank owned those records because he was the best athlete to come from Colfax," said Dockie McIntyre, Clouser's friend and teammate growing up. The school's best pitcher also started on the basketball team as a freshman, leading Colfax to the only sectional in school history (1957) before they lost to Lafayette Jefferson in the second game of the regional.

"We're not there without Frank," McIntyre says.

In addition to playing basketball and baseball, Clouser participated in Future Farmers of America and the school's play as a freshman. And that was after being responsible for farming 62 acres of land by himself.

"If there's anything I learned from my father, it's the respect you gain from work ethic," said his son, Andy Clouser, a senior manager in the international tax department for Chrysler. "That was crystallized to me in 1999, when he and I stopped unannounced in a small diner in Colfax before the Michigan State-Purdue game. At least two dozen people came to see him in less than an hour. He worked hard to earn his life."

Colfax went undefeated in 1960, and Clouser was the Hickories' winning pitcher in a 1-0 victory over Frankfort in the Clinton county championship. After he graduated with 13 others, Colfax closed and Clouser was playing baseball at Butler University. He didn't see much action, but a 1961 trip north made a big impression on the tall kid from a small town.

"We went up to Detroit to see a doubleheader between the Yankees and Tigers, and there were 50,000 people at the stadium," Clouser said. "The Tigers won both games and it was an electric atmosphere. I didn't come from a lot of money, so seeing a big city with lots of nice neighborhoods and schools made an impression. I knew this was somewhere I could move to and make a good life for myself."

After graduating in 1965, Clouser landed a science teaching position in a junior high school in Redford, Michigan. But while playing in a recreation basketball league a few years later, a teammate encouraged him to apply for the open physical education job at Kimball. The day he was hired in 1968, his new athletic director had a big job for him.

"The first thing Chuck Jones told me is, 'I want you to get the baseball team away from football coaches," Clouser said. "They're not treating the other kids fairly. The entire team is made up of football players.'"

Instantly, Clouser had made an enemy.

"The first day Paul Temerian saw me, he was walking off the football field and shouted, 'Frank, I don't like you already!'" Clouser said. "We later became good friends, but that's how I met our football coach."

Hired to coach baseball and be Jones' assistant in basketball, Clouser was replacing Herb Deromedi, who left for Central Michigan and became a College Football Hall of Fame inductee as the winningest coach in the history of the Mid-American Conference. Meanwhile Clouser limped to just 14 wins over his first two seasons, hardly a Hall of Fame beginning.

"I didn't know what I was doing. I had no philosophy or anything," Clouser said in that 1982 interview with McCabe. "But through going to clinics and listening to people speak, I developed a philosophy."

By the mid-1970s, Clouser owned Michigan's most feared program by playing "small ball" 40 years before the term became commonplace.

"When you're going up against a Steve Howe or Bob Welch you need every run you can get," Clouser said. "When we got a leadoff hitter on, I had to find a way to get him to second. In one game against Dondero, we got the leadoff hitter on and we bunted nine consecutive times – every one of them was a sacrifice or a suicide squeeze – and they screwed every one of them up. They had a good team and a good coach in Bill White, and we still scored six runs in the first inning. White was so upset, he screamed at me, "That's not baseball!'"

Despite coaching decades prior to baseball's current SABERmetrics obsession, Clouser applied statistical trends in the game to match his strategies.

"I went over our games for the last nine years and discovered that the team that scored first won 88 percent of the time," Clouser said in that 1982 *Free Press* profile. "I think we bunt more than any team in the state. Sometimes we bunt just to give (our opposition) the opportunity to make mistakes."

No opponent implemented a strategy so relentlessly as Kimball, and because Clouser's catchers spent every day in practice defending these strategies, they were more successful than most at holding runners on and throwing out runners trying to steal. It's been almost two decades since Clouser left coaching but his position hasn't softened.

"I tried to win on talent the first couple years and didn't win," Clouser said. "I couldn't score runs from first base. Steal, bunt or hit and run, but move runners into position to score. Once we got the freshman and junior varsity coaches teaching our system, the kids succeeded every year."

To mirror his own competitiveness, he turned every drill into a competition to install a pride and determination in his team.

"I worked our kids hard so they would say to themselves, 'I work too hard to lose this ballgame,'" Clouser said.

But to call Clouser just a coach and paint him as obsessed with winning would be to ignore his love of the game and willingness to share it with friend and foe alike. No one knows this better than Seaholm's Todd Siefken.

"Coach Clouser ran the tennis operation at Royal Oak's Red Run Golf Course where I played, and he was the one who taught me how to throw a curveball, among a lot of others things he taught me about baseball," Siefken said. "He was a great guy to be around and talk to. I have fond memories of Coach Clouser and owe a lot of what I was able to accomplish in the game as a pitcher to him. As opposing players, we knew Coach Clouser didn't take any shit, and we respected him for it. And he won."

He won 546 games, 14 SMA titles, 11 district championships, four regional titles and was a perfect 4-0 in state semifinals at Kimball. In four different seasons, he was named Michigan's high school baseball Coach of the Year, and in 1983, Clouser was one of eight finalists for the national award by the National High School Athletic Coaches Association after being named the District 4 Coach of the Year for Michigan, Illinois, Indiana and Ohio.

A year after that honor, Chuck Jones came to Clouser with another request: take the open head coach's position for either girls or boys basketball. While Kimball's boys program had won eight district titles and a regional under Chuck Jones, the girls' program was notoriously poor — they usually won no more than a game or two each season — but girls basketball played in the fall in Michigan back then, so Clouser took that job. The team began to win more, slowly at first, but within a few years, he was consistently averaging 12 to 15 wins a year.

A decade later his girls were on the doorstep of a perfect season at 19-0. They owned a double-digit lead entering the final five minutes against Troy in the last game of the regular season. Troy's subs were sitting at the table to finish the game when the Colts rallied, and Coach Jim Maley pulled back his replacements. Kimball wilted and a few minutes later, the game and the perfect season was lost for good. Clouser's still mad about it, describing the sour finish as, "The worst game I ever coached." Still, it was a remarkable accomplishment for a program that was pitiful just a decade earlier.

Although he continued to coach the girls' program through his retirement in 2000, his tenure as Kimball's baseball coach ended when he resigned the position unceremoniously following the 1995 season. A brief return to coaching at Troy Athens netted two more league titles in three seasons before he hung his No. 19 uniform up for good after the 2001 season.

The man who had a plan for almost everything that happens on a baseball field has a few opinions on the Miracle Maples, too.

"Seaholm always had talent – they won their share – and Don (Sackett) and I always had good games together, but they weren't always fortunate in the state tournament," Clouser said. "They had to play us or Brother Rice or some other good team. It was very hard to get out of the district. In 1988, we had great kids on our team, and that's why we won the league, but we didn't have great pitching and that's why we weren't good enough to win the state championship."

"Seaholm came back four or five times in the seventh inning to win games, so that's very unusual, because pitching almost always wins you the state championship."

Now 75, Clouser still watches the Tigers almost every night. He shakes his head at strategies he sees as counterintuitive to winning. Trying to hit the ball over the shifts and out of the park — coded by terminology like "launch angle" and "exit velocity" — directly opposes Clouser's primary theory: hitting the ball in the air dramatically increases the likelihood you'll be put out; hitting the ball on a line or on the ground increases your chances of reaching safely.

"I don't know why major league teams don't bunt more," Clouser said, the old intensity ramping up quickly. "If I'm going against Clayton Kershaw or Justin Verlander, I know I'm getting one run, two at the most. Why wouldn't you bunt in the first inning, with the idea someone's going to bloop a hit somewhere or make a mistake defensively?"

But in typical Clouser fashion, he quickly deadpanned.

"But you can't keep anyone because of the salaries, so I'll be dead before the Tigers are good again."

In the years since he retired, Royal Oak has had three coaches, but only one had to follow the legend. That was Brian Gordon, now athletic director at Novi High School. After five years under Clouser as a junior varsity coach, Gordon spent 11 seasons as Kimball's coach and another four when the school became Royal Oak High School. His teams went 311-189 while winning two league championships, five district titles and two regional titles. The student applied many of his mentor's same principles.

"I know there were times when other teams could not figure out how Royal Oak Kimball or Royal Oak High beat them because they might have been more talented, but it was because we out-worked them," Gordon said, himself a Hall of Fame coach since 2011. "I was thankful we were able to carry the torch and were able to be competitive. Frank built the baseball program at Kimball. It was his baby."[2]

---

2   Jim Evans, "Brian Gordon's baseball career earns him state HOF induction," *Daily Tribune*, June 29, 2011. Retrieved from dailytribune.com

CHAPTER EIGHT:

A STRANGE START

IN MARCH OF 1988, NO POLL OR NEWSPAPER PREDICTED SEAHOLM

to achieve anything significant. The best preview the Maples earned was penned by Marty Budner in the *Observer & Eccentric* while previewing the entire prep baseball season. It hardly spawned championship dreams.

————

"Over at Seaholm, veteran coach Don Sackett begins his 25th season in charge of the Maples. With seniors Todd Siefken, Mike Carroll and Rob Kaye, and junior Chris Kauth in the lineup, the Maples should give league favorites Royal Oak Kimball and Ferndale all they can handle."

————

In their hometown newspaper, Seaholm didn't get mentioned until page two, below the fold and not until the 10th paragraph. Ouch.

In Royal Oak, the *Daily Tribune* had predictably instilled Kimball as the leader in the SMA. The *Detroit News, Detroit Free Press* and *Oakland Press* followed suit, pegging Clouser's team as one of the teams to watch. Sackett was never going to be mentioned in the same sentence as Clouser, because the Maples had never won a district title.

Seaholm opened April 3 by sweeping Groves, then defeating West Bloomfield and Southfield before mercying Troy, 13-3, two days later. Seaholm showed their longball proficiency in that game, as Carroll, Siefken and Glandt hit back-to-back-to-back homeruns and the stunned Colts fell apart. The Maples scored four in the fourth and five more in the fifth to turn a 4-3 lead into a 10-run laugher.

Meanwhile, Kimball opened by dropping both ends of a doubleheader to Birmingham Brother Rice. Later they would lose as 7-4 decision to Cranbrook-Kingswood, a private, well-to-do Class D school that had no business taking down a program of this stature.

Seaholm was rolling; Kimball was reeling. Was this the year the Maples could punch through? Following an outstanding junior year, Siefken had firmly entrenched himself as the team's ace, from both an effort and proficiency standpoint. The preacher's son had closed the Southfield win by striking out five of six hitters and started the Troy game in dominating fashion. But there was something else about the win over Troy. Two Maple errors had allowed the Colts to take a 3-1 lead in the second inning of that game. In 1987, the Maples would have imploded, but Siefken kept his cool, and after his teammates hit three straight dingers, he put the clamps on the Colts over the last three frames.

But like a car driving down the road too fast, the quick start skidded into a ditch April 9 when Ferndale visited Seaholm. It was a day typical of Michigan's slow-to-start spring — cold, blustery and uncomfortable — but if you're a high school or college team trying to complete the games on your schedule, you play.

Coach Annis Joseph's Eagles clobbered the Maples, 16-9, turning the game into a glorified practice by coming back from a 5-0 deficit to score the next 16 runs.

Before Ferndale had five outs, Seaholm scored five runs, and the outsized Maple ego was overflowing. The Eagles regrouped, scoring two runs in the second and another three in the third. In the fourth, a tie game turned into a jail break. Siefken came in to pitch and plunked two hitters. A throwing error by Carroll was followed by a ground ball going through Glandt's legs at first. Ferndale began to tee off, sending three straight balls to the fences. As Maple outfielders chased scorched baseballs, Eagle runners churned around the bases, chasing each other home. This continued until it was 16-5 in the fifth. Tables turned, it was Ferndale laughing, mocking the Maples from their bench.

Seaholm avoided the 10-run mercy rule by scoring a pair of runs in both the fifth and sixth innings after Ferndale had emptied its bench. All of it evoked memories of Carroll's tirade a season earlier when the Troy bench erupted in laughter.

Something else grabbed Sackett's attention in the aftermath of this loss. During the handshake at home plate, before they boarded their bus to 9 Mile and Pinecrest, Ferndale had returned the smug smiles offered them earlier. Curiously, the Maples took their lumps. A season ago, the team might have added to the insult of an already ugly effort by trying to get the last word in. Instead, Sackett watched his Maples pry the bases from the infield, grab the field tools and prep the field for another day. As Ferndale's bus pulled away, the Maples stayed behind, and the silence was unmistakable.

Sackett thought to himself, *"This is a good sign. Losing is supposed to sting."*

He didn't realize it in the moment, but he had changed, too. A year ago, Sackett might have zinged his team with the intent to shame them. In 1988, these Maples were ashamed and the coach didn't have to say a word. If Sackett had to change his ways to achieve his goals, his players were learning the same lesson courtesy an embarrassing blowout.

Sometimes losing has more benefits than winning, for player and coach.

During the next two days, practice was spirited in anticipation of facing Hazel Park's Joe Roa, a hard-throwing righthander and future major leaguer. The Vikings' field, nicknamed "Green Acres" because it sat across from a harness racing track, was named for Bob Welch, who pitched for 17 major league seasons and won the 1990 Cy Young Award. There was at least a half-dozen scouts in the stands, each of them carrying a notepad and a radar gun. None of them were there to see anyone from Seaholm.

If the Maples relished the thought of stealing the show, it wasn't immediately obvious. It started to resemble the rout from a few days earlier. The Maples flailed helplessly at Roa's vicious fastballs. Newton, who always put a dollop of mustard on his own act, was being pounded. The Vikings jumped out to a 4-0 lead. Green Acres was buzzing, Roa was dominating, and the idea that Seaholm's early success was a fluke was starting to surface.

But as horses galloped peacefully past the centerfield fence, Seaholm rallied furiously late down the stretch. Opening the sixth, one base hit followed another. A double steal and then a double down the line plated two runs. Suddenly Roa was no longer invincible, and the entire bench seemed to soak in the prevailing attitude: *"Hey, we can hit this guy."* Roa came back to strike out Siefken and Newton, but Carroll reached when he beat out a ball that barely got past the pitcher between first and second. That brought up Glandt. From the bench and later, the on-deck circle, he had watched Roa throw four-straight first-pitch fastballs.

Glandt thought, *"He's going to throw me a fastball and I'm going to crush it."*

Sure enough, Roa unleashed a 95-mph fastball, a beautiful pearl right down the middle of the plate. Like a python uncorking his taut stance, Glandt plowed through it with vicious energy, sending a missile soaring into the sky.

"That was the day I started covering my back foot in dirt to stay planted in the batter's box, to make myself turn my hips and hands through the ball," Glandt said. "I hit that fucking ball to Ferndale."

Hazel Park's center fielder knew it, too, abandoning his push back towards the fence after just a few strides. He knew what Glandt knew the instant he turned his back to the plate: the ball was uncatchable. It easily soared past the fence, carrying past the horse's track, too. The game was tied, and Seaholm's bench erupted. "Joe Roa, my ass!" Newton shouted as he congratulated Carroll and Glandt.

In the bottom of the sixth, the Vikings would rally to re-take the lead, 5-4, but Seaholm's thunder carried into the seventh. Roa was replaced, and in a matter of minutes, the Maples put six more runs on the board. Hazel Park went meekly in their final turn, and an improbable, come-from-behind 10-5 win was reality. In a matter of minutes, with a triple, home run and six RBI, Glandt had stolen the show from a future major leaguer.

That most of the scouts had stuck around to see how the game ended was something the Maples took great pride in, too. Sackett told the team he was proud of how they hung in against Roa when the game started horribly, and called out Siefken specifically for "pitching his tail off late in the game." Newton re-entered the game to close out the Vikings in the bottom of the seventh to pick up the save. He'd started and had been roughed up early, but came back in to even the score, so to speak.

As the bus rolled north up Woodward Avenue, Sackett took notice of another emerging quality: resilience. The Maples hadn't thrown the towel in after they fell behind earlier. The same fight they had shown against Ferndale, easier to dismiss when you're down 16-5, had played out in the thrilling 10-5 win. His team celebrated after the wins over Southfield and Troy, but they were quiet after the Ferndale loss. "*Have they finally turned the corner?*" Sackett asked himself quietly. "*Do they respect the difference between winning and losing? If they're craving this winning feeling, that's a great sign."*

Beating Roa was significant. The Maples had stared down by a beast, pushed him off the hill and came back to win. The bus crackled with talk of how the Maples had rocked the SMA's best pitcher. It wasn't entirely true, but Sackett wanted his guys to be confident. *"If that's why they're winning, then they are, and I'm not going to take it from them."*

But before that thought had a chance to clear his consciousness, one player started talking openly about a doubleheader at Kimball. It was Newton. "Dude, we're going to kick their ass into submission!" Sackett thought, *"Of course it is."* With a worrisome look on his face of a father who knows his kid has wandered fearlessly past a dangerous boundary, he pulled his guys back in place.

"I love the confidence, but we need to take care of business first," Sackett said. "We celebrate after Kimball, not before."

The rumble quieted back down to a buzz. Kimball's rotten start was history; they'd rattled off five straight wins. They were pitching their second-tier pitchers and winning those games easily.

Clouser had set his rotation to make sure Sackett and the Maples got his two best pitchers, Darren Clark and Fred Higgins. It would be everything Seaholm could handle.

From a talent standpoint, he knew his Maples were good enough, but what separates the accomplished from the hopeful is the confidence to finish. His team had failed their first test at Ferndale. What would happen to his team's confidence if they went belly-up versus Kimball?

Don Sackett stopped his mind from racing right there. *"One dragon at a time,"* he thought. *"We'll find out soon enough anyway."*

CHAPTER NINE:

TODD GLANDT

Class of 1988, Birmingham Seaholm

WE ALL WEAR MASKS. WE SHOW THE WORLD WHO WE WANT TO

be, but our masks protect us from being revealed for who we really are.

Todd Glandt's mask is thicker and heavier than most. After the experience of Miracle Maples faded, life began for all of them. Among those 15 Maples, life happened most to Glandt. He could be your brother. Your cousin. Your uncle. A fraternity brother. A neighbor. The guy you watch the game with while knocking down a few cold ones.

This profile is not a judgment. Success is fragile. Things like death, divorce and drug abuse cause inconsolable heartbreak. The effects cascade upon everyone near the epicenter of whatever is unfolding. They divide loyalties. Cause estrangement. Tear down entire generations of families as fast as a tsunami washes out your town. What once was is forever no more.

These are things call life's tragedies. Some of these things ripped my Royal Oak-based family apart at the seams. They've ripped apart some of Glandt's life, too. Nothing immunes us from or teaches us about what happens next when bad things happen to good people. It's one of life's little secrets; you only realize that axiom as truth after it happens to you.

He protects himself in subtle, curious ways. When he says, "I'm an open book," what he's saying is, "Be gentle with me and my story, because it still hurts." When he tells you, "I don't care what people think," he's telling you, "I've been hurt too much to let you know just how much I care."

Glandt has enjoyed some incredible life experiences. He's partied with Charles Barkley, palmed Dick Vitale's head and jet-setted across the country with a Michigan basketball legend. His deft but quiet stroke helped sell properties including fast-food franchises, auto repair dealerships and multi-million dollar gentlemen's clubs. He's endured a lot of heartbreak, too, some self-induced, all the kind of tragedies that can make you question everything in your life, good and bad.

What if his marriage hadn't ended in divorce? What if he wasn't estranged from his two daughters? What if, just a decade ago, metro Detroit's economy hadn't collapsed? What if the death of his brother and sister-in-law hadn't happened? What if nothing had gone wrong? What if something else goes wrong?

Todd Glandt no longer asks those "what-if" questions. They only haunt him. Some scars are more visible than others, but he's hopeful to write another, better chapter of his life. Spend some time with him and you'll see he's got some blood in his eye, but he smiles, and his wit remains sharp, sometimes to a fault.

"As I tell the ladies at work, they don't call me 'Horse' because I'm fast," Glandt says.

He's part of a unique fraternity who, over six weeks, won 16 games in a row and embarked on one of the most improbable title runs in the near-50-year history of Michigan's state tournament. Many this brotherhood has gone on to become lawyers, accountants or captains of sales and industry. Glandt's not part of that club. Glandt, a former business broker, now waits tables at Big Rock (formerly Norman's) in Birmingham. While he hasn't closed the door on going back to his former white-collar life, he's okay with where he's at more than anyone.

Some days, the grind is longer than others. Every day, the struggle is real, but he doesn't care who's in the judging mood. The bills still need to be paid.

"At first, it was hard because there's such a stigma on being a service professional, and this is an area that houses so many power brokers," Glandt said. "Taking care of friends and even some teammates took a toll on me. I had to come to terms with what I'm doing, accept my life and let those who feel the need to judge me do that without it affecting me. It took some time to get to this point."

Like anyone who's waited tables, he figured this would be a short-term job. It's been nine years. He likes the work and he's good at it. So he stays. And it's still light years from his more humble, rustic beginnings.

"I was born in Cheyenne, Wyoming — I think I was conceived during Rodeo Week — my mother was out there for Frontier Days. She was from Minnesota, and my Dad was from Nebraska. When Nebraska and Minnesota get together in Wyoming, you get me."

It didn't take long for his mother, Sandee, to realize there wasn't enough in common with his father, Larry, to forge a longer-lasting relationship. After a divorce, she met Ed Battier. They soon married, and in 1975, this newly-formed family moved from Minnesota to Michigan, where Ed was taking an executive job managing a transportation division for Rockwell International. Glandt finished kindergarten in Minneapolis and started first grade in Birmingham.

In a region long resistant to progressive intones, a blended, interracial household was still a very taboo concept within Oakland County and well-to-do Birmingham. But if it was something to talk about for the neighbors, it was no big deal to Glandt and everyone else in his home.

"I never noticed any problems about it, although it certainly wasn't commonplace in Birmingham 30 to 40 years ago," Glandt said. "We might have been the only household like that in Birmingham."

Almost immediately, Battier began coaching, immersing Glandt within the sports community that the 'Miracle Maples' would eventually blossom from. This was when Glandt met many of his future teammates, years before they arrived together at Seaholm.

"It's true that the city of Detroit was almost exclusively black, and the suburbs were almost exclusively white in the 1980s, but at the time it didn't occur to me that Todd's dad was black, because Mr. Battier had been my T-Ball coach," Sheckell said. "He was just one of the parents who were around us all the time. I see it in hindsight where the schools in the area in general are much more diverse today than they were back then. My son graduated from Birmingham Groves in 2017 and it's very different than what I experienced (at Seaholm). That's a good thing."

As Glandt entered high school, he tried his hand at a number of sports. Because he played for the Birmingham Lions and Royal Oak Chiefs, he went out for freshman football at Seaholm.

"I caught a touchdown at Southfield. Ran a fly pattern, got past my man, caught the ball in full stride and outran him to the endzone," Glandt recalls, his face beaming at outperforming the usually faster Blue Jays, if just for a brief moment in time. He tried wrestling, too, competing while in junior high school at 96 pounds the first year and 126 pounds the next, even going undefeated one year.

But as an athlete, he wasn't naturally gifted like younger brothers Shane and Jeremy Battier. He wasn't fast. He couldn't jump with the same coordination and skill. But he toiled, often with no one watching until suddenly, his naturally soft hands and long reach made playing baseball, and specifically first base, an ideal fit for his abilities.

"Todd Glandt was the perfect first baseman," Sackett said. "He was tall, rangy, left-handed, could scoop the ball out of the dirt and he worked hard."

And his lithe frame, barely 160 pounds, conveniently hid the fact no Maple, pound for pound, hit for more power than Glandt. His ability to uncoil and send the ball to the fences almost uncanny; when it all came together for the Maples in 1988, Glandt played a starring role.

"Glandt, Kaye, Kauth and Milius were our hitters, Siefken and Newton handled most of the pitching, Carroll and I were puzzle pieces, but it was Todd who had a fantastic senior year," Sheckell remembers. "While it was all coming together for us, there was a stretch where he carried the team offensively."

And watching it all happen was the proud papa. Among spectators watching Seaholm's home games from "The Hill," Ed Battier was popular with players and parents. He had previously coached at least half of the Maples in various youth sports around Birmingham.

"I didn't have a perfect childhood — who does? — but I never found it difficult, to be honest with you, because Dad and Step-Dad was always the same thing to me," Glandt said. "Ed was always there. He was the coach, the provider, so I never thought about the whole blended family thing. Ed never adopted me, but he never had to, either. He was always 'Dad.' I still call him that. I love that man."

As Todd was starring with the Maples, his younger brothers were lurking, literally. Sheckell might have been the tallest high school second baseman in Michigan, but Shane Battier *was* the tallest Little Leaguer in Michigan.

"I had nine years on Shane, so after I graduated, I umpired Little League baseball, and they stopped games on the surrounding fields when Shane came to bat," Glandt said. "Obviously, everyone wanted to see him hit, and no one wanted to get hit when the ball came over the fence, either."

Like the rest of the Maples, Glandt didn't receive a concrete offer to continue playing baseball after high school. Finding something to substitute for the emotional high baseball provided proved difficult. So Glandt turned to the business world to mirror the challenges and thrills he found in athletics.

He was well-suited at pulling parties together, first as a mortgage loan officer, and later as a business broker, a fancy name for an agent representing the real estate interests of existing businesses. Meanwhile, Battier won the Naismith Prep Player of the Year award at Detroit

Country Day (1997), and later, the Naismith College Player of the Year award at Duke (2001). Battier was drafted by the Memphis Grizzlies in the same year, and when he wasn't making deals happen, Glandt suddenly had a first-class window into the NBA roadshow across the country.

Jeremy and Ashley Battier, Todd Glandt and Shane Battier in 2014.
(Todd Glandt collection. Editor's note: A previous edition of this book incorrectly identified Ashley Battier as Shawna Battier. The author sincerely regrets the error.)

Back in Birmingham, Jeremy Battier was making a name for himself as an outstanding football player at Country Day. When the Yellowjackets won the state title in football, a hat trick of state championships among the brothers in the Battier household had come true.

Todd helped lead Seaholm to a baseball title. Shane headlined back-to-back state basketball titles at Country Day. Jeremy was a champion in football. It's a legacy few households could ever imagine, much less fulfill. And impossible to sustain in any context.

The problems started in 2006. He endured a divorce from his wife of seven years, the custody, property and support mediation process wrecking him emotionally. He became estranged from his two daughters, then nine and six years old. His father, Larry, 70, died in Minneapolis. Certainly not the goodbye he envisioned.

"I would go back and see him once, maybe twice a year," Glandt said. "I got divorced and my father died in the same year. I remember it like it was yesterday."

In 2008, as if being staggered by the near-collapse of the American auto industry wasn't enough to bear, metro Detroit was flung head-first into the mortgage and investment banking meltdown. In the tri-county area, issues that had plagued Detroit for decades were suddenly everyone's problems. While people were walking away from homes they couldn't sell for the price of a VCR in the city, homes that typically sold for between $300,000-400,000 were suddenly available for $150,000 or less in the suburbs. Some of the region's enclaves were facing 50 to 60 percent foreclosure in both commercial and residential sectors. Some families moved in the middle of the night, the shame of foreclosure making a formal goodbye to neighbors impossible to bear.

Almost overnight, the deal maker had no deals to make, no business to broker. Without the income he needed to not only live, but to satisfy judgments, Glandt turned to waiting tables at Big Rock.

But his fight against the forces pulling his life apart wasn't over. More bad news arrived August 9, 2015 when Jeremy Battier was found dead of a fentanyl overdose in a Cincinnati hotel room. He had followed Shane to Duke, played football, and after graduating earned his MBA. After a long stint as an executive at Cincinnati's Horseshoe Casino, he was serving as president of Seven Star, his wife's upscale, boutique dental practice.

Fentanyl, a pain reliever for cancer patients, is 50 times more potent than heroin. Inexplicably, it's often mixed or laced with heroin. A single dose can be deadly, and Hamilton County (Ohio) law enforcement officials believed it was the first time he had tried the drug, or possibly a combination of the two.

The effects of drug abuse are devastating but like a car crash, it's something you don't truly understand until you've experienced it first hand. Nothing is as it was before, no matter how hard you try to fix it and a loss of this magnitude is sometimes unfathomable.

So you can imagine the shock the family endured when just 60 days later, Glandt's sister-in-law, Shawna Battier, died of a fentanyl overdose, too.

"That remains the toughest event in my life to date, and it's something I'm still not over," Glandt said.

Don't judge Todd Glandt. He wants to fix what's broken but who knows how or where to start? How do you fix what's been broken for so long? Who knows how to fix your life when there's so much of your life to fix? Things like a good education, professional success, personal wealth and social status mean nothing when life breaks and suddenly, nothing is as it was. Still, he endures. He goes to work. He meets with friends. He finds satisfaction with small, simple successes. They take some of the sting away, if just for a few hours.

"I was an extra in the *Batman Versus Superman* movie — Officer Brenner for the Metropolis Police Department — and I was the only one in the scene who wasn't a cop in real life," Glandt says, before telling of a commercial he did for a Memphis barbecue restaurant with Battier and Pau Gasol, though he admits he never actually saw the finished product.

"I had a bit of a resume going," he says with a wink, revealing his desire to keep things light

86

No one would blame him for having hardened more than most to life's fires. He's not lost sight of what he can do better. He'd like to fix his relationship with his daughters, Emma and Ally, now 21 and 18, even if he doesn't know how he'll do it.

"What else am I going to do?" Glandt asks. "That's the only way I know how to go through life. I've got to be me."

CHAPTER 10:

TWO COUNTRIES

AN EMERGENT THEME OF PRESENT-DAY DETROIT IS HOW HARD

the surrounding suburbs fight to claim ownership in Detroit's comeback story. The irony is most of these communities have spent the majority of the last 50 years trying to distance themselves from the state's signature city.

Today, there's two different Detroits to visit: the popular downtown visited by millions and populated by thousands of millennials, and still-desolate neighborhoods ignored by the resurgence. But from 1988, Detroit and the suburbs were two different countries. In a book celebrating an improbable high school championship 30 years ago, it's important to recognize what the region was and how it is slowly changing to gain a perspective of the importance role high school sports plays in defining the neighborhoods and cities the schools represent.

By the 1980s, membership in the SMA created odd, sometimes awkward socio-economic dynamics. The eight members were situated along the north-south corridor of Woodward Avenue in south Oakland County. Hazel Park and Ferndale, the two most southern schools, comprised blue-collar, middle-class communities. Hazel Park was almost exclusively white and often called "Hazel-Tucky." Ferndale was emerging as an oasis for school kids trying to escape Detroit's troubled public schools, and Southfield, notable as a "minority-majority" school in mostly white Oakland County. Every day, hundreds of teens crossed the 8 Mile Road border down Pinecrest into 'The 'Dale." Meanwhile, the two most northern schools, Seaholm and Andover, represented two of Michigan's most affluent zip codes. Birmingham's 48009 holding the distinction for the most foreign car registrations. Troy was emerging upper middle class, while Berkley and Kimball, dominated by post-World War II salt boxes, sat in the middle. It wasn't a melting pot, and diversity wasn't always accepted among these neighboring communities.

While not as pronounced as it was 30 years ago, divisions between black and white dominate metro Detroit. These divisions allowed the city to fall into disrepair while suburbs like Birmingham and Royal Oak rose.

Spread across three counties and including Detroit's massive, 140-square mile footprint, a staggering 117 different, incorporated communities duplicate civil, social and educational services every day, week, month and year. Some of these communities are magnificent. Most are respectable, working-class enclaves of a formerly mighty industrial center. Some are blighted beyond imagination. This is what has pitted cities against suburbs, defined post-World War II America and fueled dramatic and devastating population shifts since the 1950s.

The only tragedy in Detroit's comeback is it should never had to happen at all.

Once the wealthiest city in America on a per capita income basis, Detroit began suffering a massive wealth transfer starting in the 1950s that would skip over Detroit and reinvest itself in the suburbs. Today, eight of the 10 wealthiest zip codes in metro Detroit are from Oakland County.[3] Birmingham and Bloomfield Hills took three of the top four places on the list. Over the same time period, nine of metro Detroit's 10 poorest zip codes are now located inside Detroit's border.[4]

---

3   Benjamin Raven, "Metro Detroit's top 10 richest ZIP codes," Feb. 24, 2017. MLive Media Group, retrieved from www.mlive.com.
4   Benjamin Raven, "$21,000 to $294,000: Metro Detroit's enormous wealth gap broken down by ZIP code," Feb. 25, 2017. MLive Media Group, retrieved from www.mlive.com.

Metro Detroit's wealthiest zip codes	Metro Detroit's poorest zip codes
1. 48304 (OAK. Co.; Bloomfield Hills)	1. 48212 (DET; Hamtramck)
2. 48302 (OAK. Co.; Bloomfield Hills)	2. 48211 (DET; Poletown)
3. 48009 (OAK. Co.; Birmingham)	3. 48213 (DET; East Side)
4. 48301 (OAK. Co.; Bloomfield Hills)	4. 48238 (DET: West Side)
5. 48025 (OAK. Co.; Bev. Hills/Franklin)	5. 48210 (DET; West Side)
6. 48168 (WAYNE Co.; Northville)	6. 48228 (DET; Warrendale)
7. 48323 (OAK. Co.; West Bloomfield)	7. 48342 (Pontiac; OAK. Co.)
8. 48070 (OAK. Co.; Huntington Woods)	8. 48205 (DET; East Side)
9. 48236 (WAYNE Co.; Grosse Pointe)	9. 48204 (DET; East Side)
10. 48363 (OAK. Co.; Oakland Twp.)	10. 48209 (DET; Southwest)

Detroit's decline allowed the dramatic rise of suburban high schools. Today, the ethnic populations that comprise metro Detroit's suburban high schools look nothing like they did 30 years ago. In the late 1980s, city schools were predominately black and suburbs schools were almost exclusively white. It took Michigan's one-state depression (2000-09) the largest municipal bankruptcy in U.S. history (City of Detroit, 2013) to start to reverse this dynamic. The financial services bubble bursting and the mortgage crisis of 2008 forced this region to accept diversity within large swathes of neighboring bedroom communities.

Conceptually, it's simple: decade by decade, the transfer of whites out of Detroit multiplied exponentially, bulging the cities that made up the outer-ring communities of Detroit. Two in particular, Royal Oak and Birmingham, were transformed from sleepy bedroom communities into emergent cities with four high schools and powerhouse athletic programs.

In the Census year 1940, nine percent of Detroit's population, then over 1.6 million, was black. Royal Oak, just two miles from Detroit's 8 Mile border on Woodward Avenue, was nearly all-white and estimated at 25,087, almost 10 percent of Oakland County's total count of 254,068.[5] By 1950, Detroit was well past 1.8 million residents and the black population (300,506) had nearly doubled. In Royal Oak, the migration north had grown the city by 87 percent, to 46,898.

Automobiles and airports replaced trains and trolleys across the country as President Eisenhower's Federal Aid Highway Act bill effectively allowed concrete valleys to be poured through neighborhoods. In Detroit, those neighborhoods were predominantly black, and the effects were breathtaking.

Most major U.S. cities were built on the backs of immigrants, but Detroit's immigrants were for the most part domestic, Southern-raised blacks and whites, the prejudices born of their southern upbringing always simmering beneath the surface.

"You had the wealthiest black per capita living in Detroit, Michigan, and (it was) because of the auto industry," said screenwriter Barry Michael Cooper, whose observations of Detroit were the basis of the 1991 movie *New Jack City*. "(Autos) had everything to do with that migration from the South to Detroit, Michigan. It was more affluent than Harlem, actually. It was stable. We're making cars, and everyone needs to drive."[6]

With white population migrating north, affordable housing hard to find and compounded by unfair lending practices, blacks were penned into overcrowded neighborhoods, causing the landscapes of city high schools to transform almost overnight. A prime example of this is Detroit Central High. Once dominated by Detroit's Jewish population, Central became a majority black student body, while whites and Jews re-populated at Detroit Mumford, which opened in 1953. Detroit Miller High, popular and successful, closed in 1956.

---

5   Detroit Free Press, *Geography/Beyond 8 Mile/Oakland County: The Detroit Almanac*, 302
6   *American Gangster: The Chambers Brothers*. BET. Dec. 26, 2006

Demographers believe the city population peaked at close to 2 million in about 1953,[7] but Detroit was the fifth-largest city in America in 1960. Detroit's Catholic High School League boasted 64 schools sponsoring football, but schools in inner ring communities were becoming de facto powerhouses. Royal Oak High had split into Kimball and Dondero, Birmingham High had become Seaholm and Groves and these schools were either on the doorstep or well past the threshold of 2,000 students.

As Detroit hemorrhaged thousands of workers, these new suburbanites brought student enrollment and tax revenues. In the two decades after World War II, the Big Three automakers built 25 new plants in suburban areas outside the city.[8]

This expansion allowed the SMA to roar to life in 1964 when, along with Berkley and Southfield, Seaholm and Kimball joined Ferndale and Hazel Park in leaving the Eastern Michigan League. What they left behind was long bus trips and historic rivalries with East Detroit, Port Huron and Mt. Clemens.

This kind of change was happening everywhere in metro Detroit. And then a volcano exploded at 12th and Clairmount, a neighborhood nestled between three major freeways due north of downtown and Midtown. Sunday, July 23, 1967, a disturbance in the early morning darkness turned into an uprising by dawn; it was a full-scale riot by mid-afternoon.

That Sunday, the Tigers would split their doubleheader with the New York Yankees, and as the final out was recorded, the city shook with the first of several seismic shifts that would decimate Detroit. Rioters smashed windows and left behind rivers of fire 10 blocks long.[9]

The Tigers were next scheduled to host Baltimore, but as the riots spiraled further out of control, the team instead traveled to Baltimore.

---

7   Detroit Free Press, *Geography: The Detroit Almanac,* 289
8   *American Gangster: The Chambers Brothers.* BET. Dec. 26, 2006
9   *A City on Fire: The Story of the '68 Detroit Tigers,* HBO Sports, July 22, 2002

Some Tigers, particularly those who lived within minutes of the ballpark, objected.

"I get a call from the traveling secretary, and he says, 'You gotta be on a bus. We're going to Baltimore,'" said Jim Northrup, a Tigers outfielder from 1964-74. "I said, 'What makes you think I want to go to Baltimore? I have a family here. They're killing people! They're burning down the town!'"[10]

It lasted five gruesome days, and the numbers still astound: 43 people died, 7,000 more were arrested and 2,500 buildings had been looted or destroyed beyond repair. The riots, spread out over 25 square miles of the city, redefined everything physically, socially and culturally.

No street symbolized the 1967 riots in Detroit more than Pingree. Brick homes were burned into dust, and like so many other neighborhoods, this street never recovered after 25 square miles of the city were devastated. (*Author collection*)

"I think that there was just no turning back from the damage that the riots of '67 did to Detroit," said George Cantor, a sports writer at the *Detroit Free Press* from 1966-69 and later the *Detroit News*. "In the

---

10   *A City on Fire: The Story of the '68 Detroit Tigers*, HBO Sports, July 22, 2002

years that followed, the riots never stopped. Crime, the homicide rate, the rate of white departures to the suburbs kept on spiraling, kept on going up and up. My parents moved during that winter...moved out to the suburbs after spending their lives in Detroit. There was just this sense among the white community that 'Detroit' was over."[11]

The riot turned 8 Mile Road into Detroit's de facto Berlin Wall for the next 50 years.

"You started to hear it then, and you still hear it today — people who claim they don't cross 8 Mile — Eight Mile being the northern border of the city of Detroit," said Tiger fan and Detroit resident Jim Grossman.[12]

The physical and psychological wounds, created by the riot, remain omnipresent on the national conscience within pop culture movies like *8 Mile, Gran Torino, Detroit, White Boy Rick* and *The Mule.* Media like this celebrates the violent tendencies that have rarely slowed since 1967. Only twice has Detroit finished a year with less than 300 homicides: 2015 and 2017. In 1968, the total shot up more than 100, from 281 in 1967 to 389. At the high water mark in 1974, Detroit had 714 homicides.[13]

Paige Northrup-Smith, the daughter of Jim Northrup, says her family lived in Detroit in 1967. A year later, they did not.

"I remember we moved from a corner house on Crosley, at the beginning of the street. It was a cute little brick bungalow. There was a fence and maybe an overpass," Northrup-Smith said. "In the spring and summer, we always ate dinner early because Dad had to go to the ballpark. We often went to the games. After the riots, we lived in Bloomfield Hills. The Kalines lived near us, too. We were in the new house when the Tigers won the World Series (1968). Dinner started

11   *A City on Fire: The Story of the '68 Detroit Tigers,* HBO Sports, July 22, 2002
12   *A City on Fire: The Story of the '68 Detroit Tigers,* HBO Sports, July 22, 2002
13   James David Dickson, "Detroit has lowest homicide tally in 50 years," Detroit News, Jan. 1, 2018, retrieved from www.detroitnews.com

earlier because the drive to the stadium was much longer. We didn't go to games as often."

The Northrup family, like most other Tiger families and thousands of Detroiters, relocated to Oakland County and visited the city less frequently after the 1967 riots. Jim Northrup (center) played 11 seasons for the Tigers before finishing his career in Baltimore; his daughter to the right, Paige Northrup-Smith, lives on Maryland's Eastern Shore across the Chesapeake Bay from Annapolis, Md. *(Northrup family collection)*

By 1970 Detroit's overall population tumbled to 1,511,482 while Royal Oak had almost 8,000 students attending four high schools, an incredible increase of 237 percent over 1950. Further north along Woodward Avenue, Birmingham's four high schools, Groves and Seaholm plus Catholic schools Brother Rice and Marian were similarly flush.

The mountain that exploded in Detroit found its way to Oakland County in August 1971. Pontiac, the seat of Oakland County government, is still derisively jeered as "Ponti-Black" by the region's racists.

On an oppressively hot and humid evening, just a few days before the city's schools were set to open, a hole was cut in a six-foot wire fence and dynamite was placed atop the fuel tanks of at least six buses parked along that fencing. A fuse was lit, and seconds later, 10 school buses exploded in a blistering wall of fire, while another three were damaged.

Pontiac, a city of 84,000 similar to Flint, was decidedly blue-collar with almost half of its citizenry employed at the Fisher Body or Pontiac assembly plants. Like Detroit, Pontiac's black population had swelled since the 1950s, and the schools had rapidly changed, too. But Pontiac's not-so-subtle leadership was resistant. While some blacks had moved into virtually all-white neighborhoods, most of the city's black population lived in the over-crowded south side of the city. The sheer volume created ghettos that resembled the big city dilapidation found in Harlem and Brooklyn.

A 1969 complaint filed in federal court sought relief for what was described as deliberately segregated schools. The brief detailed how Pontiac's schools were either 90 percent white or black. An open occupancy law did little to integrate the racially-polarized neighborhoods and schools. When a state-of-art high school (Pontiac Northern) was scheduled to be built to address overcrowding at Pontiac High School (later renamed Pontiac Central), its location was overtly placed in an all-white neighborhood. Ultimately, the city placed the new high school near the city's downtown after a number of staged protests; it did little to relieve escalating tensions.

The complaint landed on the docket of Damon J. Keith, who ruled Pontiac's school board intentionally perpetuated segregation and ordered the city's schools to bus pupils to the school of their choice to achieve integration by the fall of 1971. As had happened in Detroit, whites fled, and the district lost 11 percent of its student population.[14]

---

14   Patricia Zacharias, "Irene McCabe and her battle against busing," *Detroit News*, May 3, 1997, retrieved from detroitnews.com

But the fiery explosion and the endless appeals of Keith's decision from a group calling itself National Action Group (NAG) — led by Irene McCabe, a 36-year-old housewife and represented by L. Brooks Patterson — ultimately failed to stop the forced busing. The arsonists later identified as Ku Klux Klansman, were caught and convicted. The media glare left and Pontiac's exodus eventually slowed.

Scenarios like this played out in other big urban centers in the late 1960s and early 1970s around the country, but none more so than Detroit. As thousands of residents left the city over two decades, the pool of qualified leadership drained away, too. Poor decision-making, coupled with feelings of abandonment and hopelessness accelerated Detroit's problems. As a byproduct, a number of athletic events became platforms for violence and racial strife, invading the safe haven high school sports represented as a forum where blacks and whites could set aside their differences for an afternoon or evening.

In 1972, Dondero left the Border Cities League, abandoning rivalries with Grosse Pointe South, Wyandotte Roosevelt, Monroe, Dearborn Fordson and Highland Park for comparable, local competition in the Metro Suburban Athletic Association. There were finally enough schools for Dondero to fill out a schedule within a much smaller radius, eliminating the need to drive into and through Detroit, yet another example of how city and suburban schools were able to isolate from each other.

The decline of Catholic schools available in the city became more noticable, too. Catholic Central relocated to Breakfast Drive in Livonia in the late 1970s, the occupancy of their old building on Outer Drive assumed by Detroit Renaissance, a public school. Detroit Austin closed. Detroit DeLaSalle would abandon their eastside legacy near the city's airport for a new campus in Warren in the early 1980s.

When the 1980s arrived, massive blight in the industrial and residential sectors, and crack cocaine began further ravaging Detroit.

"When a city of 140 square miles loses half of its population, and a considerable portion of its tax dollars, blight and abandonment rapidly rise. In 1989, *Free Press* reporters traveled the more than 2,500 miles of city streets and counted 15,215 vacant structures, including 9,017 single family homes, 225 apartment buildings and 3,414 vacant businesses. The city estimated then that up to 200 structures a month were being abandoned in Detroit."[15]

The city issued just 13 single family home building permits in the entire decade; many of the abandoned homes became dens for the production and distribution of crack.

"This is a city that had more guns than residents — that's the starting point — and then you put crack cocaine into this mix?" asked Chris Hansen, a news reporter at Detroit's WXYZ before becoming nationally-known for his work on NBC's *How to Catch a Predator.* "It was explosive."[16]

The narrative in the suburbs was decidedly different. Michael Kaline, son of the Tigers' Hall of Fame right fielder Al Kaline, graduated from Bloomfield Hills Lahser in 1980. Northrup-Smith graduated from Andover in 1981. Troy, Rochester and Rochester Hills emerged as newer and upscale, while automotive, advertising and accounting executives continued to seek posh addresses in Birmingham, West Bloomfield and Bloomfield Hills as well as the Grosse Pointes. When I-696 opened in 1987, Royal Oak's Main Street was redefined, and the city has enjoyed a reputation for a must-visit nightlife destination for nearly 30 years.

The mainstream media tagged this slow-moving tsunami as "White Flight," conveniently ignoring the fact that blacks were fleeing the city in search of better neighborhoods and schools and more value for their tax dollars, too. That pilgrimage is best exemplified by two brothers, Greg and Ray Kelser. Nicknamed "Special K" before he graduated, Greg Kelser was a *Detroit Free Press* All-Public School League basketball performer at Detroit Henry Ford before joining Earvin "Magic" Johnson at Michigan State.

---

15   Detroit Free Press, *Geography: The Detroit Almanac*, 294
16   *American Gangster: The Chambers Brothers.* BET. Dec. 26, 2006

Ray Kelser, eight years younger than Greg, didn't follow. Instead he attended Southfield High, where the Blue Jays set the SMA's record for consecutive league wins with 32 and reached the Class A Final Four in back-to-back seasons.

Exclusively white and Jewish in the 1960s, Southfield is another example of how fast some Detroit-area high schools changed. In 1971, the first year of the state baseball tournament, Southfield's two public high schools reported just six black students among an otherwise all-white student count of 4,751. Just five of Southfield High School's 2,426 students were black — that's 0.206 percent — and at Southfield Lathrup, one black student joined an otherwise all-white student body of 2,331.

Southfield: A place to start over?

Southfield's two schools, nearly all-white in the early 1970s, were majority African-American by the mid-1980s. The city was a destination of choice for blacks and whites alike fleeing Detroit in search of better schools, neighborhoods and property values. *(Detroit Free Press)*

By 1985, of Southfield's 1,607 students, 852 were black and 775 were white. Lathrup, meanwhile, had increased their African-American student count to 253 out of 1,652.[17]

Part of a handful of schools then identified as "minority-majority" in mostly-white Oakland County, the Blue Jays were an outstanding

---

17   Dawson Bell, Lona O'Connor, "Southfield: A place to start over?" Detroit Free Press, Aug. 8, 1985.

SMA contributor, especially in football, basketball and track and field. And the city's business center was bustling as a de facto replacement for white collar offices that had long ago left Detroit. But those successes didn't always warrant a warm welcome, says Galen "Rick" Duncan, who played basketball at Southfield from 1982-86 before playing at Lake Superior State University.

"I attribute a lot of the things I heard on the floor to gamesmanship to gain competitive advantage, because we said things, too," says Duncan, "but it was what was said or implied off the floor that made things uneasy. Because of the stares from parents and kids, we knew when we walked into the gym we weren't always welcome. The kid from Seaholm or Andover could wear their varsity jacket in downtown Birmingham or on Orchard Lake Road in West Bloomfield and attract a presence for themselves. We knew wearing our jacket in the same places would attract a police presence. There were a lot of places we knew we couldn't go."

The ridiculous assignment of a person's value being based on a zip code continues today.

"Even when I introduce myself as 'from Detroit' to other blacks, I'm sometimes asked where I grew up, and when I say 'Southfield' I sometimes get labeled as 'one of those people,'" says Duncan, now working as the Vice President of the Kings Academy and Professional Development for the Sacramento Kings after 10 years of fulfilling a similar role for the Detroit Lions. "It's something that makes me feel so frustrated, I really can't put it into words."

Detroit's suburbs continued to expand in flat, horizontal waves. The auto industry's slow hemorrhage of jobs and the ancillary work that followed it — Tier I, II and III-level suppliers, accounting, advertising and engineering, as well as uniform supply, dry cleaners and diners — were closing. Families who could afford to move in Oakland County first went to Berkley, Ferndale, Southfield and Royal Oak. The next wave went to Birmingham and Bloomfield Hills. A third wave rolled over Troy, Rochester and Rochester Hills. In the last decade, Lake Orion and Clarkston have emerged as the larger, newer and more exclusive communities to matriculate to.

For decades, headlines like this November 7, 1986 'Black Friday' story in the morning edition of *Detroit Free Press* defined the narrative of the American auto industry for millions of metro Detroiters. A near-bankruptcy in 2008 nearly toppled General Motors and Chrysler.

Like a big wave that washes away much of the beach it rolls over, what was left behind was paltry in comparison. By 1990, Kimball was at just 1,194 students, a drop of over 66 percent from what it had been in the early 1970s. Meanwhile, Seaholm was at 1,103 and eventually dipped to 985 students by 2000, playing for a handful of seasons as a Class B school.

Almost 30 years later, Royal Oak has closed, re-purposed or torn down a dozen schools. Construction cranes dot the city's downtown skyline, erecting parking structures, office buildings and newer, trendy bars. They represent millions in investment from private and public sectors. In the last decade, Ferndale and Hazel Park have been recast by offering similarly affordable retail and residential properties as Royal Oak had earlier. But not everyone sees the growth as a positive. In the spring of 2018, the letterboard at Como's, a now-closed pizzeria at Nine Mile and Woodward in Ferndale, read, "Don't Royal Oak my Ferndale!"

In the 30 years since the Miracle Maples' championship run, many of the schools Seaholm called rivals have closed. In fact, on Seaholm's 1988 baseball schedule, 10 of the 27 games came against seven schools no longer in existence. Kimball and Dondero merged to become the Royal Oak Ravens in 2006. Pontiac Central and Northern became the Pontiac Phoenix in 2009. Bloomfield Hills Andover and Lahser combined into the Bloomfield Hills Blackhawks in 2013. Southfield and Southfield Lathrup melded into Southfield A&T Warriors 2014. On the day of the 30-year anniversary of the Seaholm's state title, Taylor Kennedy's final class graduated.

In Detroit, city rivalries like Cody and Cooley disappeared when Cooley closed in 2012. Detroit's Redford and Mackenzie have disappeared. Catholic League stalwarts like Notre Dame and Bishop Gallagher in Harper Woods, St. Florian in Hamtramck and DePorres and Benedictine in Detroit are gone, too. Even Farmington Hills Harrison, home of the most prolific football dynasty in Michigan, is scheduled to close in June, 2019.

Some powerhouse schools across remain. Brother Rice in Birmingham. Detroit Catholic Central in Wixom. Lake Orion and Clarkston. Diversity is now much more accepted than it was 30 years ago, evidence West Bloomfield becoming "minority-majority" without much of the stigma that would have been assigned 30 years ago. Some of the ills of past leadership remain too. L. Brooks Patterson remains Oakland County executive, although his seven-term reign will end on Dec. 31, 2020 because he has stated he will not seek re-election.

What's noticeably different is Detroit and the suburbs are no longer permanently resistant to a progressive landscape that seemed unimaginable 30 years ago.

No matter how or why it happened, what was lost in a micro sense — rivalries decades ago between dozens of schools that have been re-named, repurposed or closed altogether — has been offset by the macro changes across the region that are too often overlooked: the metro Detroit region is slowly making socioeconomic progress.

It's true the success and failure of the auto industry continues to define the region. It's also true successes tend to be modest and failures remain devastating. On the Monday following the 2018 Thanksgiving weekend, General Motors announced it would cease production at the Warren Transmission plant, the Detroit-Hamtramck plant — the plant Detroit allowed GM to build in the early 1980s after bulldozing the Poletown neighborhood utilizing eminent domain in the same manner they built the freeways in the 1950s — and plants in Baltimore, northeast Ohio and Ontario, Canada. The Black Monday news put in peril the jobs of 8,000 salaried employees and 3,300 hourly workers.

The Hamtramck plant built the Chevrolet Volt. When the company was on the verge of bankruptcy in 2008, this was the vehicle General Motors used as point-to evidence the automaker was still a nimble, tech-savvy savant, not a bloated, top-heavy creation of three decades of bad decision-making. We heard the bailout was going to be worthwhile, in part because the Volt was proof of GM's capability to bring to market a cutting-edge technology to compete with Asian manufacturers. But 10 years later, GM ditched the Volt for the Bolt, a slimmed-down version of the Volt assembled at a plant in Detroit's suburbs, while letting the last plant it owns inside Detroit's borders to go dark in 2019, like so many other facilities have before it.

It's far from fixed — the domestic auto industry or metro Detroit's social climate — but the region is slowly figuring out how to co-exist instead of exist in spite of one another. It's a remarkable change for a region constructed ostensibly to resist such changes.

CHAPTER 11:

WALKED OFF

ON FRIDAY, MAY 5, 1988, AT ROYAL OAK'S MEMORIAL PARK, THE chance to take down Kimball and win the SMA for themselves arrived for the Maples.

Waiting for the Maples inside that opposing dugout wasn't a typical Clouser team. Kimball had been proven beatable in a stretch of inexplicable losses, before reviving their season with a handful of victories two make this doubleheader a true showdown. That was fine with the Maples; they had no problem with curb-stomping a hated rival when they were down.

The weather had evolved into a nearly perfect spring day in Michigan. A bit chilly in the morning, a mix of sun and clouds gave way to a light breeze, and the high reached almost 70 degrees. In Game One, Seaholm took control early and led most of the game. Kimball was able to stay close because Mike St. Peter homered and singled in another run. Eventually, the Knights came back to tie the game in the seventh and force extra innings, but in the top of the eighth, the Maples got to Kimball pitcher Darren Clark and grabbed an 8-6 lead.

But in the bottom half of the eighth, Newton struggled to get ahead in the count. Forced to throw strikes in the middle of the plate, Kimball started one of their trademark rallies. Gary Homberger tripled to open the frame. The Knights got another runner to second before Mike Mossoian singled, scoring both runners to tie the game. Worse, when the Maples tried to to cut down the tying run at the plate, Mossoian took second as the winning run after trailing most of the game.

Matt Newton got by on guts and guile, and these attributes made up for his lack of natural, raw talent or refinement by coaching. His determined approach led to six wins and a save in seven state tournament games. *Photo by Dan Dean (Hometown Life)*

Newton now faced Mike Siwajek, Kimball's quarterback the past two seasons and a recruit to Kalamazoo College to play football and baseball. The left-handed first baseman laced the first pitch into right field on one hop, and Mossoian was running the instant the ball pinged off the bat. Cam Mueller, playing shallow because there is no home run fence in right field at Memorial Field, uncorked a throw but Mossoian easily won the race home.

Kimball began spilling out of their dugout in celebration 30 feet before Mossoian touched the plate.

"*Fucking Kimball,*" Newton thought as he started to walk off the field, a mixture of disbelief and anger beginning to boil inside him. "*Did this really happen? What the fuck!*" Now, as Newton reached Seaholm's dugout, the 17-year-old exploded, slamming his glove on the metal bench in frustration, creating a loud reverberation as he screamed, "Are you fucking serious?!!"

Sackett took a much more stoic approach to the moment. He'd seen Kimball complete this kind of comeback dozens of times over the years. This was what worried him while coming home from Hazel Park on the bus. Newton had gushed in enthusiasm in anticipation of a victory over Kimball, but he didn't have a plan if something like this happened. Sackett's response muted the outrage, even if it didn't change the outcome on the field, and was the kind of guidance he received little if any credit for.

"Our day was over right there," Carroll remembered. "That was as pissed off as I remember our guys. We hated Kimball. Losing to them, like that, was the worst possible outcome. But it gave us a taste in our mouth that we resolved to never taste again."

Kinkade remembers a different narrative.

"There was a lot of ego on the field that day. We knew we were good and when we came back to steal that game, I think Seaholm wondered a little bit if their success was real," Kinkade said. "There's a confidence that comes from the success we had for as long as we did at Kimball, and that's probably why were able to come back we had done that so many times. We expected to win, right down to the last strike."

This was Kimball's primary advantage: the ability to win a ballgame in which they might not have had the better talent because they were well-schooled and fundamentally sound. Seaholm's anger was raw and real because they let Kimball off the hook and they knew it.

The victory was win No. 400 for Clouser. Amid the celebration, someone from Kimball retrieved the ball Mueller had thrown from the outfield and handed it to Clouser.

Jim Evans

Frankly, he's the best

ROYAL OAK — If baseball coaches put notches in their belts, the thing Frank Clouser uses to hitch up his trousers would be God-awful looking.

Four hundred and one scratches. Four hundred and one man-made blemishes. Heck, Clouser couldn't even pay the Salvation Army to take it off his hands.

Four hundred and one gunfights on dusty infields at

EVANS

high noon or a few ticks later. Four hundred and one opponents left twitching in the batter's box.

Clouser's teams at Royal Oak Kimball have won one state championship. They have been runner-up in Class A three times. They have been 10 district titles and 11 Southeastern Michigan Association championships.

Kimball sweeps

Royal Oak Kimball's baseball team swept a doubleheader from Birmingham Seaholm on Friday, giving Coach Frank Clouser his 400th and 401st career victories at Kimball. See Page 11.

has a 10-year-old daughter, Jennifer, and his son, Andy, is eight years old.

How many players has Clouser had? How many names has he had to learn? How many faces has he had to recognize?

You figure it would be all be one big collage by now. All the Johns and Joes and Jims must be blending in together into one unrecognizable mass.

All the faces over the years must have evolved into one mass of eyes, noses, teeth and pimples.

"I remember all of the players," said Clouser. "Maybe some of the ones who didn't play too much I don't remember as well, but I try to recall them all.

hot shots grow up. They start wearing varsity jackets. They win.

But they graduate. No talent this year, shrugs the coach. It's .500 or worse. Nothing I can do about it.

Clouser doesn't like to rely on fate. He doesn't like to wait for the occasional fat pitch down the middle from the gene pool. He doesn't like to wait for the second coming of Babe Ruth.

His teams win regardless. Some years the Knights boast the likes of Brad Havens or Jim Kosnik. Other years it's Pee Wee Herman and Barney Fife. But the victories still come.

"Frank's a teacher," explained Don Brownie, who has been his assistant coach for eight seasons. "He's much more than a coach."

All those notches don't just appear. All those wins don't just happen to be loitering around the diamond at Kimball.

"We spend a lot of time on the mental aspect of the game," said Clouser. "Discipline has always been very important. The kids know if they screw up they aren't going to play.

"A good ballplayer is both a master of

Frank Clouser's 400th and 401st career wins earned him a profile in Royal Oak's *Daily Tribune* after Kimball swept rival Seaholm.

"I don't remember the specifics of that game because after all these years – the games blend together more these days – but the ball marked as the 400th win is still sitting in my den," said Clouser, now 75. "We won a lot of games late like that, so I'm not surprised when you tell me how it ended."

Kimball took an 8-2 decision in the second game. Homberger hit a two-run home run, St. Peter knocked in two more and Kinkade slammed the door to close it out for Kimball. The comeback in the first game was the fourth SMA game the Knights had won in the late innings, and the *Tribune's* Jim Evans profiled Clouser, who spun that folksy aura that followed him to Royal Oak from Indiana.

―――――

The occasion called for champagne. Frank

Clouser was leaning towards a frozen

Coke. … "I'm not much of a drinker," said

Clouser, who is in his 21st season at the

helm of the Knights. "My brother did give

me a bottle of Dom Perignon for helping

him stain his house … I'll probably just stop

on my way home and get a frozen Coke."

———

Kimball was losing games it won easily in previous years, but in the eyes of the local media, this was little more than an aberration. On the bus ride back to Birmingham, Sackett wasn't overly concerned with losing. As was the case in so many previous years, he figured he'd get another shot at Kimball in the district playoffs.

"My Dad used to preach all the time that we had two seasons; the league season and the state tournament," Mark Sackett said. "If the league season didn't work out, there was a state tournament to get ready for. Of course, some years that wasn't an optimistic goal, but there was an edge to that team in 1988. You see the teams in your district during the regular season or in a league game, so no one sneaks up on anyone."

CHAPTER 12:

STEVE KINKADE

Class of 1989, Royal Oak Kimball

EVEN THOUGH HE'S LIVED IN SUBURBAN OAKLAND COUNTY SINCE the early 1980s, Steve Kinkade is, at his core, a city kid.

The former Royal Oak Kimball basketball and baseball star grew up a few blocks from Denby High School at 15460 Mapleridge in Detroit. The home hasn't been part of Kinkade's life for 35 years, but he re-discovered it in 2018, finding it tucked inside a five-part series from the *Detroit News* called "Death by Instagram." The feature detailed how rival gangs use violence and social media hand-in-hand to control drug trade on Detroit's East Side. The home's zip code, 48205, is now one of the poorest in metro Detroit, a formerly great neighborhood now ravaged and war-torn.

It wasn't always like this. Back in the late 1970s and early 1980s, Kinkade had a bike and lots of friends.

"While my parents were at work, I'd be miles — and I mean *miles* — from my house every day with my friends," Kinkade said. "Back then my street was all brick homes and big trees, side doors and milk chutes, and a garage in the back. No one worried. It's not like that now."

These days, Kinkade spends his days behind the front lines of the multi-billion dollar American car business. As decisions big and small come across his desk, his responsibilities — creating and guiding narratives as an automotive public relations executive for the Honda and Acura brands — tower over the more carefree days he enjoyed 30 years ago at Kimball.

117

Some of what he learned back then guides him on good days, and occasionally haunts him on others. One lesson in particular stands out: the future of your company and your own legacy is at risk every day your competition is better than you. Kinkade saw it play out in real time in 1988, watching Birmingham Seaholm win one of Michigan's most improbable state titles. Within the auto industry, others learned that lesson in 2009, when Chrysler and General Motors were failing so badly, they required massive injections of government assistance to survive.

Kinkade's inclusion in the middle of the Miracle Maples' story is a commentary of how life happens to all of us. How we all want something better for our kids than we had growing up. How success and failure is sometimes unburdened by color, gender or money. It's a reminder that in failure or tragedy, there's always room for lessons learned and future success.

Life began to change for Kinkade sometime between his sixth and seventh birthday when his mother, Marilyn, divorced her husband, an axel assembler for Ford Motor Company. A couple years later, she had to check herself into a hospital to battle cancer, so Steve spent the summer months of 1980 in Birmingham. There he would earn a nickname while foreshadowing changes that would alter his family's history forever.

"I stayed with my Uncle Jim and Aunt Sharon Beshke," Kinkade said. "Their son, my cousin, was C.J. Beshke, and he was a baseball star for Seaholm. He played for the Berkley American Legion Post team and I went to most of his games that summer."

The Berkley post team was coached by Ferndale alum Mark Monahan and was comprised of the best players from Berkley, Hazel Park, Kimball and Seaholm. Besides Beshke, the Maples' Greg Lotzar and Ray Ziegler, plus Kimball pitcher Dave Kopf, shared starring roles.

One night, C.J. asked his eight-year-old cousin if he'd like to be the team's bat boy. Berkley won that night. Steve continued on as the team's bat boy; the team continued to win. Towards the end of the season, Marilyn Kinkade had improved enough to return home to Mapleridge, and she was ready for her youngest son to join her. But there was a problem. Since Kinkade's first appearance as bat boy, the team had rattled off 13 straight wins and given him a nickname: "Teddy Bear." Because baseball culture is filled with crazy superstitions, if you believe your team is winning because a kid nicknamed 'Teddy Bear' is your bat boy, then you are.

"Someone on the team drafted a letter — it almost read like a petition — asking Ms. Kinkade to allow her son to stay with our team for the remainder of the season, and every player signed the letter, too," said Monahan, who left coaching soon after and has been a scout for the Detroit Tigers for almost 30 years. "A kid who felt like he was part of the team was in a tough spot and our guys loved him for it. 'Teddy Bear' made that season memorable."

So Marilyn Kinkade acquiesced. 'Teddy Bear" stayed with the team and Berkley went all the way to the state final before losing to Midland, 3-2. Kinkade returned home to his mother and two older siblings in Detroit. Soon thereafter, his mother left her administrative assistant's position at Guardian Angels Catholic School — the site is an empty lot today — just blocks from her home on Mapleridge for a similar position at an automotive supplier in Royal Oak.

Like Greek city-states, metro Detroit is layered with complexities. Your zip code often reveals as much about your Detroit heritage as your last name. Are you an East Sider or West Sider? Are you from the Pointes? Downriver? Do you attend Catholic school or a public school? It was expected that generations of the same family attended the same schools.

While paying Catholic school tuition for three kids in Detroit, Marilyn Kinkade was getting a daily dose of why Royal Oak enjoyed a reputation for affordable housing, great schools and parks and outstanding recreational programming. So like Ray Kelser attending Southfield instead of Henry Ford, it was a break in the ranks when a single mother relocated her family in 1983 from Detroit's east side to Royal Oak, from Wayne County to Oakland, from Catholic schools to Kimball.

"She'd grown up in Grosse Pointe. Graduated from Dominican High School. Our entire family, Mom and Dad's sides combined, was either from the eastside of Detroit or Grosse Pointe," Kinkade said. "She wanted what was best for her family and was determined to deliver. It's a decision I have the utmost respect for today."

It's a decision that splintered the family. Kinkade's older brother, Dave, was attending Detroit DeLaSalle near Detroit's City Airport when the school relocated outside of the city to Warren in 1982. Instead of moving to Royal Oak, he moved in with his grandmother to finish at Harper Woods Bishop Gallagher so he wouldn't have to leave his friends on the eastside.

Kinkade's sister, Colleen, was scheduled to graduate from Harper Woods Regina in 1984, but instead graduated from Kimball in 1984. Steve spent 8th grade at St. Dennis in Royal Oak and was enrolled to attend Madison Heights Bishop Foley High School. But after playing in Royal Oak's summer baseball league and winning the Kaline League World Series in 1985 as a 13-year old, he developed strong friendships with the Royal Oak kids on the team with him. That convinced him to ask his mother to enroll him at Kimball instead. A powerhouse in both football and baseball — most often compared to Bishop Gallagher when it came to the best Class A baseball program in metro Detroit — Kimball's rivalries with Ferndale, Seaholm and Dondero were well-documented, too.

Kinkade entered high school expecting to contend for league and state titles, but four years later, the big stage he envisioned was a big disappointment. Like his family, like his former Detroit neighborhood, Kimball was changing.

"It wasn't the same school I grew up reading about in the *Daily Tribune* or *Detroit Free Press*," says Kinkade. "A lot of our best coaches had retired or were finishing their teaching career."

Almost overnight, Kimball's football team was routinely being hammered by schools it had dominated for decades. In basketball, Chuck Jones left Kimball's bench in 1984 for his new role as school and all-city athletic director. Gary Fralick, who went 72-35 at Redford Thurston, was hand-picked as Jones' successor. He inherited Dan Kosnik, a junior and the best player in school history. No one thought Fralick would struggle — especially with a star like Kosnik — but following a legend is difficult, especially at a school suffering a rapid decline in student enrollment. Fralick went 34-54 (.386) from 1984-88, winning just five games in each of his last two seasons.

Kinkade played a prominent role on those teams. He was pulled onto the varsity as a sophomore and helped Fralick break a 14-game losing streak by scoring 16 points against Hazel Park. The team finished the 1986-87 season at 5-17, Fralick ralling his team to a second-straight district final before losing to Sterling Heights, 52-51.

The next year, Ferndale, Seaholm and Troy battled for the SMA title while Kimball endured a 5-16 season. While players like Ferndale's Dewayne Stephens and Sheckell battled for All-League, County and State honors, Kinkade was distraught about Kimball's dismal record. His playing time had dwindled to almost nothing midway through the year, in his eyes part of a bigger, systemic problem.

"We were terrible. Many of us were frustrated with not mixing up the lineup to see if we could get a spark," Kinkade said. "The reality is we had good players on that '87-88 team — Mike Ries, Paul Link,

Gregg Morrison, Mike Siwajek among others — but we lacked chemistry within a rotation that never changed."

Frustrated, Kinkade called Fralick after returning home from practice to ask what he could do to help change the team's performance and get more minutes. Fralick's answer was a dagger through the heart.

"Gary told me he didn't see me as an asset to have on the floor in key situations, words that stung quite a bit since I'd been moved up to varsity as a sophomore," Kinkade said. "Being a 16-year-old with the propensity for a knee-jerk reaction, I skipped practice the day after that conversation and quit the team."

The next day, Jones called Kinkade into his office.

"He asked if I would go back on the team for the rest of the season and I said, 'Yes.' In reality, I never wanted to quit, but was very frustrated and didn't want to waste my time if I couldn't make a valuable contribution to the team," Kinkade said. "Mr. Jones was doing the only thing he could do for his coach in the short term. I didn't want Kimball to keep losing, so I agreed to come back, but I didn't see much playing time for the rest of the season. Gary sent a message to me that he didn't want to be shown up."

A 65-52 loss in the first round of the state tournament to University of Detroit Jesuit ended the season at 5-16, and Jones called Kinkade back into his office.

"He asked if I would play for Gary as a senior and I said, 'No,'" Kinkade said. "I appreciated Mr. Jones listening to my concerns that matched the concerns of many others on the team at the time. Gary was no longer a good fit for our team."

Moving on might have been the best thing that happened to both of them. Although the team's record didn't improve much, Kinkade returned to the program as team captain under new coach Tom Daniels and was named Kimball's most valuable player and All-SMA, too.

Fralick re-emerged at Troy High School, where he's won five district titles and nearly 300 games (292-239) through 2017-18. He won his 350th game overall in 2015 and is scheduled to win No. 400 in December of 2018. He's coached his two sons, Gary, Jr. and Timmy — Troy's all-time leading scorer, a handful of All-State players and James Young, who has played with the Boston Celtics and Philadelphia 76'ers.

Fralick's 25-year tenure at Troy and overall record of 398-328 (at time of publication) at three schools make his coaching career an unqualified success, but neither Fralick nor Kinkade got the return they sought at Kimball.

But unlike Fralick, Kinkade had baseball to fall back on, a sport Kimball still dominated. With 30 years of perspective, Kinkade's view of the Miracle Maples has changed in some respects, and it hasn't changed at all in others.

"Seaholm winning the title in '88 still sucks," Kinkade says. "We were shocked in 1988. In the moment, we didn't fully grasp the opportunity we had before us. We took a lot of things for granted after having such a successful regular season and winning the SMA."

"Today we realize because they won it all, they get the well-earned credit. We had the same opportunity and blew it."

That it was Seaholm only made it worse.

"We didn't like them and they didn't like us. There were so many great rivalries in the SMA at the time, and Seaholm was a great rival. We had our list of people we'd love to throw at and I'm sure they had theirs," said Kinkade. "That Seaholm team was so cocky and arrogant and they really had no reason to be during that '88 season. We were the better team, but they were the team that went out and got it done in the playoffs, which is really all that matters."

After the disappointing exit from the 1988 playoffs, Clouser coached a summer travel team comprised mostly of his own players, including Kinkade. That team dominated, winning 22 of 23 games and the Oakland County title before losing in the playoffs to teams made up mostly of college players. But summer baseball doesn't generate the same interest and the accomplishment went unnoticed. In 1989, Seaholm got the last laugh again by winning the SMA and sweeping both games from Kimball. They eliminated the Knights from the state playoffs in humiliating fashion, a 17-9 decision in the pre-district game. Matt Newton was the winning pitcher.

"We never recovered from Miracle Maples," Kinkade says. "After we lost to Troy, we figured Seaholm would lose in the next round. No one thought they'd win the district, the regional or the state title. Shock turned into anger at another team winning something we were capable of winning, too. For years, I couldn't look at the Miracle Maples sign on Woodward Avenue."

As talented as Kimball's 1988-89 teams were, Kinkade figured he and others would have many opportunities to play at the next level. But the level of promotion Kinkade and others needed didn't play to their coach's strengths or fit Clouser's style.

"Clouser didn't need to build his legacy — he was an established, Hall of Fame coach — and he wasn't comfortable contacting college recruiters," Kinkade said. "We had Division I talent. Darren Clark and Fred Higgins both threw in the low 90s. And I don't know of many other teams who could hit like we could. So much talent and not anything to show for it from a scholarship standpoint. We beat Joe Roa (Hazel Park), who pitched for the Braves. We beat Jason Beverlin (Dondero), who pitched for the Tigers. We beat Andy Fairman (Berkley), who played at Michigan. Why didn't Clouser promote us to college coaches more?"

If it's because Clouser didn't think they were Division I or II-level players, it would be up to them to prove him wrong. After graduation and a full rotation of summer baseball, Kinkade was offered an invite to Sante Fe Community College, a defacto elite feeder program for the University of Florida. He moved with his mother to Gainesville, Florida. But it didn't take long for Kinkade to feel exactly like what he was: a kid from Michigan swimming upstream in Florida. Just 17 years old, Kinkade was soon homesick and declared Florida a poor fit, a decision he still regrets today.

Moving back to Michigan, Kinkade made the Grand Valley State University team the following fall as a walk-on, but chronic injuries, a season of fall baseball and an endless winter training schedule extinguished his fire. He graduated from Grand Valley with a journalism degree in 1995 without so much as an at-bat.

College athletics is littered with stories like Kinkade's. You might not like the opportunity in front of you, but it might be the only one you get.

"Looking back now, there are so many things I would've done differently," Kinkade said. "But I was 17 years old. I learned quickly if you made a poor decision or don't get a break here and there, you were essentially on your own trying to sell yourself. I knew it was time to focus on school and get my life underway."

Immersing himself in a pathway to Detroit's automotive industry, Kinkade earned an MBA from Michigan State following graduation from Grand Valley, and started climbing the communication chains. First stop was Delphi, General Motors' off-shoot, before moving on to work in senior leadership roles at Audi AG and Ford Motor Company.

In 2011, after more than two years at Ford, Kinkade moved to Ally Financial. Again drawing on his experience at Kimball, time created perspective that wasn't evident in the moment.

"Leaving Ford was my decision and I left on good terms, but when you give notice to leave for another company in the automotive game, it's standard industry practice that your access to the company server, email, cell phone and building get removed quickly," Kinkade said. "It was a harsh reminder of what happens when you're no longer on the team, another lesson I point back to Kimball."

Steve Kinkade (right), pictured at Detroit's annual international auto show, celebrates one of Honda's multiple Car and Truck of the Year awards. He's leaned on his successes and failures at Kimball for guidance in his professional and personal life. *(LinkedIn/Steve Kinkade)*

Like Fralick, Kinkade's professional and personal life is an un-qualified success. He lives in Rochester Hills, 30 miles from the family's former epicenter in Detroit, in a house at least four times the size of his home in Royal Oak, light years from the shadows of Denby High School. Like his mother, he's given his children a bet-ter upbringing than he had, and because of the changes he saw his mother and siblings endure, life's successes are a little sweeter. Still, he catches himself remembering the events that did and didn't play out in 1988 and beyond.

"The overarching lesson from 'Miracle Maples' for me is you or your company cannot afford to miss your chances," Kinkade said. "In that context, my experience at Kimball was invaluable, teaching me the consequences when you give up or don't give it your best shot."

"People love a winner and a great Cinderella story — Seaholm got it done in '88 — so I won't deny them the spotlight they earned. But, maybe if we win the state championship that year, things fall into place much differently. Our team will always wonder…"

CHAPTER 13:

FINISH STRONG

SADDLED WITH THE WEEKEND TO STEW ABOUT THE LOSSES TO

Kimball, Seaholm limped past the midway point of the season, and the word 'uninspiring' would have best described the season on paper.

Considering the work they'd put in and the anticipation for the doubleheader with Kimball, there wasn't a lower point to the season. The Maples' season could have turned ugly — the last two seasons turned ugly without being broomed by their rivals — but Seaholm had played inspired baseball the majority of the season, the meltdown against Ferndale and Kimball aside. That no one else took notice was what would make the final three weeks of the season and the playoffs special.

Seaholm rallied in the final three weeks of the regular season; they would not lose again.

On May 12, the Maples took on Country Day, the school Carroll had considered his life boat. The Yellow Jackets were a contender for the Class C title since the day the season started, but Seaholm sparkled in a 6-1 victory. As the last out was recorded, Sackett was equal parts thrilled and relieved. He wanted to see a decisive response to what happened in Royal Oak, and this was the perfect answer. Because this was just one game in 25 years of coaching Seaholm, he showed the same pale-faced emotion he did on any other day, but Sackett was mindful of how his team had gone about this game. They were patient at the plate and waited for good pitches — Milius had hit two home runs and knocked in four — while Newton picked up another win on the hill. They were crisp on the field, also an indication of their focus.

Next up was Troy, a team the Maples had mercied, 13-3, in April, and they prevailed in this rematch, 8-6. After the embarrassment of the final home game of 1987, Seaholm had swept the Colts. The next day, Seaholm broomed Bloomfield Hills Andover in a doubleheader, taking the first game, 13-5, and the second, 8-3.

A doubleheader with Berkley and All-State candidate Andy Fairman, headed to play at Michigan on a scholarship, was next. This first game was a make-up of a April 27 rainout, and Seaholm lulled the Bears to sleep, pounding out an 8-2 win. Siefken started and picked up the win while hitting a double, triple and knocking in three runs. The Maples took game two, 9-6, when Kauth tripled to score the winning run in the sixth inning. Sheckell knocked in four runs on three hits, including a double and triple of his own, and Newton earned the win despite giving up two home runs to Fairman.

The only drama during the rest of the regular season came when Sackett got tossed out of a game, leaving his son, Mark, to coach the rest of the game. Today, getting run from the game would mean missing the rest of that day's competition and all of Seaholm's next day of competition, too. The next day penalties Michigan high schools are familiar are instituted on a state-by-state basis and in Michigan, the MHSAA instituted a next game penalty to accompany an ejection beginning with the 1990-91 school year. They added next day of competition — not just the next game — to the rule in 1997-98. The elder Sackett was also too sick to at coach the Berkley games, so Mark Sackett ran those games, too. The meant Crede Colgan, the team's designated cut-up, got to play. These were the only games Colgan got any playing time in all season.

A final payback was in order. Still smarting from that 16-9 loss, the Maples made amends for that with a 10-9 win at Ferndale. Kimball clinched the SMA for a second-straight season with a narrow 8-7 win over Hazel Park, a 23-9 win over Troy — that score that would play a key role in the upcoming district — and a 14-4 drubbing of Andover. Seaholm finished 15-5 overall and second in the SMA at 10-4, three games behind Kimball.

Seaholm was nothing more than an afterthought to compete for the district championship, but Sackett thought otherwise. His guys were playing well, flying under the radar and the low point of the season was behind them. The bracket draw for the district took place, and in a stroke of incredibly bad luck or fate, the Maples drew the No. 2 ranked team in the state, Southfield Lathrup, in a pre-district game. The two schools were scheduled to play May 23, but that game was immediately scrubbed after the draw in lieu of the district pairing. Both pre-district games would be played on May 27, a Friday afternoon.

No one expected Seaholm to have more than a puncher's chance to win this game, but Seaholm had quietly formed a solid, one-two pitching punch. Siefken was Seaholm's ace because he could reach the low 90's, owned a three-pitch arsenal and had an extra gear no other pitcher on the team possessed. His teammates had great respect for those abilities. But the elixir to solve Seaholm's mid-season malaise was Newton, succeeding on equal parts guts and guile. He didn't throw hard, instead pitching to contact with a pedestrian fastball that was set up by an array of off-speed change-ups and curveballs. His success was only overshadowed by the way he brazenly shot down the hitters he struck out like a gunslinger.

Matt Newton's cocky fire-brand belied a fierce drive to win and an understanding that by infuriating his opponent, they'd be focused on an emotional response towards Newton instead of winning the bigger battle for their school. *Photo by Dan Dean (Hometown Life)*

Newton had two rules when he pitched. Pound the zone with strikes, putting pressure on the hitter to put the ball in play. Second, he did everything he could to make the hitter focus on him instead of his pitches. Trying at all costs to attract the bull's attention to him and away from killing the cowboy worked, because he was 7-1 entering the state tournament, the only the loss coming from the three-run meltdown at Kimball.

"I loved watching Newt suddenly come up and pitch, and when he had a day, the way he strutted around the mound, it was fun to watch and energized the team," Siefken said. "We needed that spark because the rotation we had wasn't all that deep or solid."

Cocky would be the kind word to use to describe his antics. Newton's teammates loved it, but opponents hated him. And he knew it, too.

"I was an asshole, no doubt about it," Newton says with a laugh. "But I had to be. I didn't have great velocity, and I didn't have a guaranteed 'out' pitch, either. I was tossing junk up there, so I needed different advantages. I had to throw strikes, because the longer I was up on the mound against the same hitter, the greater the chance I'd get tagged. And making the other team hate me was crucial, because when they were thinking about me, they weren't focused on the job they had to do at the plate against Seaholm."

Carroll and his teammates knew something else was afoot.

"We realized we were pretty good. We had some assets, like our ability to hit, and our ability to bounce back," Carroll said. "We had been stunned by the way we fell apart against Kimball, but that might have been the best thing to happen to us, even if we didn't understand it in the moment. They had won the SMA, the smaller trophy. We had a chance to take the belt and steal the ring."

Still, with Lathrup looming, they had to sit on those emotions.

"That pre-district was going to be played (at Seaholm), and we had a somewhat quirky field back then," Carroll said. "Because there was an elementary school beyond centerfield, our home run fence in right-center field jutted out at a weird angle to make room for their playground. We had benches, not dugouts, and the tennis courts on the first base side left a lot of room for the opposition to foul out. We knew if we could hang around long enough, maybe we could make a game of it."

A perfect set of circumstances had arrived, and the storm it would cause was on no one's radar.

CHAPTER 14:

A MIRACLE BEGINS: THE DISTRICT

BECAUSE THERE ARE OFTEN MORE SCHOOLS THAN AVAILABLE

districts, many brackets in the Michigan High School Athletic Association baseball tournament host pre-district games to create the formal bracket. As a result, one or more schools receive a bye into the first round.

Districts are constructed on proximity and student enrollment. The closer you get to the state's population centers, like Lansing and Saginaw, Kalamazoo and Battle Creek, Ypsilanti and Ann Arbor, and especially the three-county Detroit area, the more likely you'll see pre-district games, with private and public schools paired together. In 1988, Kimball hosted a six-school district that included Seaholm, Troy, Troy Athens, Birmingham Brother Rice and Southfield Lathrup. Few districts in Michigan boasted this kind of brand-name recognition.

Lathrup, ranked No. 2 in the state, was champion of the MSAA. Kimball, the SMA champion, was expected to contend for a district and regional title annually; Brother Rice played in the toughest division of the Catholic League. Seaholm and Troy had finished second and third in the SMA, regarded as one of the toughest leagues in the entire state.

Brother Rice and Athens both received a bye, determined by a blind draw. At 20-15 overall but a disappointing 8-12 record in the Catholic League's Central Division, Brother Rice lagged far behind regular season champion Harper Woods Bishop Gallagher. Athens was rarely a contender in Oakland County or the state playoffs. The winner of Kimball and Troy would meet Athens; Brother Rice would get the winner of Lathrup and Seaholm.

Kimball hosted Troy, and Lathrup traveled to Seaholm in the other pre-district. Troy Athens awaited the winner of Kimball-Troy; the winner of Lathrup-Seaholm would meet Brother Rice.

This is the uniqueness of the state tournament at work. Schools like Kimball and Lathrup being placed in a pre-district game was akin to having to win a play-in game to qualify for the NCAA's basketball tournament. Within Michigan's high school baseball community, it was almost universally assumed Lathrup and Kimball would advance.

But Troy stunned Kimball, 12-7. Kimball's stature was built on pitching and defense over two decades, and these Knights didn't have much of either. Clouser let this Kimball team swing the bat more than ever, and they scored seven or more runs 18 times, put up 10 or more runs seven times, and won 15 of those games. The week before, during the aforementioned 23-9 annihilation, the Colts had made it easy by walking 18 Kimball hitters.

After watching his team outslug the competition to win the SMA, Clouser knew this was a bad recipe for winning the state tournament. He shared these concerns with *Tribune* reporter Mike Jordan: "You don't always win district games with good hitting," the day his Knights completed the SMA season with a 11-1 win over Berkley.[18]

Troy, just 11-10 coming into the game, stunned the Knights with a six-hit, six-run third inning. Mike Maddie's two-run home run was the crushing blow, and Kimball made some uncharacteristic fielding and base running errors. Kinkade took the loss pitching in relief.

"We played 10 good games in a row to capture the league championship," Clouser told the *Daily Tribune's* Jerry Mawhinney. "Our last game of the season was poorly played and it cost us."[19]

---

18   Mike Jordan, "Kimball finishes 13-1," Daily Tribune, May 24, 1988.
19   Jerry Mawhinney, "That was fast! Troy wins!" Daily Tribune, May 28, 1988.

Worse, the Colts were more concerned with getting to prom — seniors drove separately, leaving the bus nearly empty going back — after they ended Kimball's season.

"After the way we hammered them the week before, we didn't take Troy seriously, and it showed, obviously," Kinkade said. "In less than two hours, the season was over. I think we were so stunned it happened, it barely registered, not only after the game but that entire next week of school, too."

Seaholm had their own monstrous hill to climb, and an audience, too. The entire Brother Rice team and coaching staff came over to watch the game as an opportunity to scout the Chargers.

"There was no doubt who they were there to look at," Carroll said. "If there was one team for us to beat besides Kimball, it was Rice, and they were letting us know we didn't even register on their radar."

Lathrup boasted shortstop Alexi Gagin, who earned a full scholarship to Michigan State University, and pitcher Steve Collias, who accepted the same offer from Eastern Michigan University.

Inside Seaholm's dugout, no player was receiving so much as a form letter to gauge their interest in playing college baseball at any level.

———

May 27, 1988

Pre-District: Southfield Lathrup at Birmingham Seaholm

———

Collias started for Lathrup; Newton for the Maples. "Newt" had bulldogged his way to the top of the rotation midway through April, and for all his "talk the talk" attitude, he had walked the walk since the implosion against Kimball.

The Maples opened the game with three hits in the first inning, but inexplicably didn't score. Through four innings, the game was scoreless thanks to Sheckell, who cut down two Chargers at the plate. The first play came when Lathrup had a first and third situation and tried a double steal. When the runner at first broke for second, Sheckell anticipated the runner at third breaking for home, and had gained a large enough distance between the bag and home plate to intercept Carroll's throw and fire it back in time to allow Carroll to tag the runner out.

A few innings later, Lathrup had a runner on first when a ball was hit into the gap between center and right field. Sheckell had trapped the short-hop throw back to the infield between his thigh and the protective cup as the runner hit the bag at third and broke for home. He turned and fired home, then fell to his knees as Carroll applied the tag for the out.

"Coach Sackett came out and asked if I had hurt my arm, and when I told him what happened, he said, 'Shit, those little dingers will be fine,' and he went back to the dugout," Sheckell said.

In the top of the fifth, Seaholm finally blinked. Lathrup's Will Elkins singled up the middle. Steve Reith attempted to move him up with a bunt, which Glandt pounced on quickly, but his throw to second sailed into the outfield, allowing Elkins to move to third. Newton got a strikeout but surrendered a walk to load the bases. That brought up Gagin. With a full count, Newton's last chance missed wide. Gagin trotted to first base and Lathrup had a 1-0 lead.

David Katkowski was up next, and hit a bouncer to Kauth, who came home to force Reith. Carroll pivoted off the plate and just nipped

Katkowski at first base for an improbable 5-2-3 double play. With just one run surrendered, the inning was over.

But the Maples couldn't answer and in the sixth, Steve Memran launched a missile past the home run barrier and all the way to the Midvale Elementary School fence, to make it 2-0. The way Collias was pitching, Seaholm's season looked like it was finished.

"They were taking a shutout into the bottom of the seventh, so they were celebrating the win at that point," Sheckell said. "We certainly weren't in a good place."

Seaholm's last chance was led off by Carroll, who rocketed a double to center field. Sheckell was up next and walked. Ball four was wild, allowing Carroll to get to third. That became more important when Bret Russell, who was up next, struck out. On strike three, Charger catcher John McGlough tried to throw behind Russell to pick Sheckell off first. The throw was wild, and although Sheckell didn't advance, Carroll walked home from third to make it 2-1.

Now Newton batted for Cam Mueller, and he hit a ball with a slight Baltimore chop at Gagin. It should have been a double play to end the game but the unanimous All-State selection butchered the ball, leaving runners at first and second.

Collias fanned Siefken for the second out, bringing Glandt to the plate. Desperate to atone for the error that was now standing between the Maples and what could be a tie game, Glandt started digging his front foot in the ground and covering it with dirt to remind himself to stay rooted through his swing.

He smashed a single through the right side and Sheckell, all 6-foot-4 of him, lumbered around the bag at third and beat the throw to the plate – barely! – to tie the score.

Steve Sheckell raced home and beat the throw to score the
game-tying run in the bottom of the seventh inning against
No. 2 Southfield Lathrup. Notice the Lathrup catcher,
hurriedly trying to put the tag down, failed to secure the ball
on the throw home. *Photo by Dan Dean (Hometown Life)*

Inexplicably, an unimaginable upset was just 90 feet away. Up
came Kauth, and seconds later he slammed a single up the middle
– the 'ting!' of the bat triggering a giant shrill from Seaholm's fans
– and Newton ran home with the winning run. Greeted by a mob
scene, he thrust his index finger held high as his teammates lifted
him in the air.

The alpha moment of the Miracle Maples' run to the title: Matt Newton came home to cap a three-run rally in their final at-bat to eliminate No. 2 Southfield Lathrup from the state tournament in a pre-district game at Seaholm. It was the first of five consecutive wins by Seaholm in their final at-bat. *Photo by Dan Dean (Hometown Life)*

If Troy beating Kimball was shocking, Seaholm coming back from a 2-0 deficit to beat Lathrup in a handful of pitches was an earthquake. The second-ranked team in the state was done.

"Kauth got the hit to win the game, and even today, it still doesn't feel like it really happened," Sheckell said. "It's baseball momentum, the ability to do things you otherwise wouldn't be able to do."

Like a scene from the Walking Dead, Lathrup staggered off the field in a daze. Later, they were forced to wait for a bus sitting in disconsolate silence, the iconic images captured by *Observer & Eccentric* photographer Dan Dean.

Lathrup players are left to sulk after having their state title dreams dashed by the Miracle Maples. *Photos by Dan Dean (Hometown Life)*

"It's too bad we had to blow it all like this when all we needed was just three outs," Lathrup coach Bob Marten told Budner. "We played good enough to win, except for that last inning."

Seaholm was enjoying a huge boost of confidence in the afterlight of winning such a huge game, and in the manner they had. In the era prior to the Internet and Smartphones, news of Kimball's improbable loss wouldn't reach the Maples until the next day. As word spread, the Maples took the time to smirk, too.

"It was a game changer for us," Carroll said. "We realized if we could beat Lathrup, we could beat anyone else, too."

Seaholm's stunning victory over No. 2 Lathrup, occurring in a matter of pitches, grabbed the attention of everyone who paid attention to high school sports. *(Observer & Eccentric)*

Southfield Lathrup	(21-5)	000	011	0	-	2	4	1
Birmingham Seaholm	(16-5)	000	000	3	-	3	6	1

WP: Newton. LP: Collias. 2B: **SL** - None; **BS** – Carroll. HR: **SL** - Merman. RBI: **SL** - Gagin, Merman; **BS** - Glandt, Kauth.

———

June 4, 1988; Royal Oak Memorial Park

District Semifinal No. 1: Birmingham

Brother Rice v. Birmingham Seaholm

———

Next up was Brother Rice, which played home games at a YMCA field just west of Woodward Avenue in Birmingham. Just based on dimensions – and its 'Sandlot' appearance – it looked like anything but a facility befitting a Class A powerhouse. But for Brother Rice, the lack of facilities didn't stop Coach Ron Kalczynski from recruiting top-flight talent, and it showed with Rice's recent success in the state tournament.

With more than a week to prepare for a district semifinal, few would have blamed the Warriors for chalking up Seaholm's victory over Lathrup as a fluke. Their indifference toward the Maples said as much. The game was the first of three that Saturday, and 10 a.m. came quickly for Seaholm, which held its senior prom the night before. Newton started the game for the Maples; Jeff Calcaterra, an All-Catholic League pitcher, got the nod for the Warriors.

The game opened with three scoreless innings. Rice took the lead in the top of the fourth when Dean Moscovic notched the Warriors' first hit, a triple to left to score Calcaterra from second. Newton stopped the bleeding by stranding Moscovic at third.

In the bottom half of the inning, it appeared the Maples would tie or take the lead. Kauth and Kaye smacked back-to-back singles to open the inning, but Calcaterra roared back to fan the next three Maples. *"That might have been our best chance…"* Sackett thought, a nod to his team's past failures in the district playoffs.

A single by Moscovic and a double by Marty Moraniec were the only blemishes to follow against Newton, but the Warriors still held a 1-0 lead through six innings.

Calcaterra's work was easy and precise, and with the exception of the first inning, he'd frustrated the Maples thoroughly. But no position player knows an umpire's strike zone better than a catcher, and in the Maples' last turn, Carroll would again be the unlikely tablesetter. He'd hit sixth all season, with Sheckell, Russell and Mueller to follow. These were role players who got on base enough to triggered bigger rallies when the Maples' big bats at the front of the order came around.

Just as he did against Lathrup, Carroll reached, this time with a walk.

Sheckell struck out trying to move him over with a bunt, but Russell moved the line forward by singling to left, moving Carroll to second. Now Newton hit for Mueller, and he singled, but Sackett put the brakes on Carroll as he hit the third base bag.

The weight of winning five consecutive games in their final at-bat wore on all the Seaholm players. Matt Newton took some time to fill his head with positive thoughts before the Maples' final at-bat against Brother Rice in the district semifinal. *Photo by Dan Dean (Hometown Life)*

This decision was risky. With just two outs to spare, how many more chances would Seaholm have to plate the potential winning run? A game-ending double play remained a possibility, too. But Sackett trusted the top of his lineup, and Siefken proved his coach's trust correct by lacing a rope into left field. Carroll scored the tying run, and the bases remained loaded for Glandt.

The home run fence ended abruptly in right field at Royal Oak's Memorial Field, so Moraniec, the right fielder, was playing up towards first base to leave himself a chance to throw out the winning run at the plate. Any ball over his head would end the game.

For the second straight game, Glandt was in position to be a hero. He swung at the first pitch, slicing a fly ball to right field as Russell raced back to toe the bag at third. Moraniec, Rice's only other All-Catholic League selection, uncoiled a throw to home as Russell pushed off the bag. The throw sailed past the catcher, smashing halfway up the 20-foot high backstop. Russell won the furious, 90-foot sprint easily and the Maples began pouring out of the dugout again. Another come-from-behind win. Another mob scene at home plate.

"Oh my God, we just beat Brother Rice!" Sackett said to himself as he watched another celebration unfold.

Brother Rice walked through the usual handshake at home plate in a fog. It had all unraveled in a matter of pitches. Kalczynski, brother of Detroit Red Wings' radio announcer Ken Kal, was gracious with both the *Tribune* and *Observer & Eccentric*, telling Budner and Mawhinney: "They deserved to win. They got the crucial hits when they needed them."

From the stands, what Troy witnessed seemed impossible to comprehend. *Did we just see that...Brother Rice losing a tournament game to Seaholm?* In the span of 10 days, the Maples had knocked off No. 2-ranked Lathrup and Brother Rice.

Many of the Maples had been up into the early hours of the morning, a few had even pulled an all-nighter celebrating the prom. Exhausted, they would await the winner of Troy and Troy Athens.

Between the win over Rice and the district final against Troy, Sackett was consumed by one prevailing thought that he kept to himself: *"Don't you jokers get complacent on me now. Just because you've won a couple games and Kimball's not here to play the final doesn't mean anything. I want this district title."*

Birmingham Brother Rice (20-16) 001 000 0 - 1 0 0
Birmingham Seaholm   (17-5) 000 000 2 - 2 0 0
WP: Newton. LP: Calcatterra. 2B: **BR** - Moraniec; **BS** – None; 3B: **BR** - Moscovic; **BS** – None. RBI: **BR** - Moscovic; **BS** - Glandt, Siefken.

June 4, 1988; Royal Oak Memorial Park

District championship: Troy v. Birmingham Seaholm

In the other semifinal, Troy staged a mini-miracle of their own by scoring three runs in the top of the seventh to stun rival Troy Athens, 5-2, and the Colts would give Seaholm everything it could handle.

Jeff Bates started for Troy, while Sackett countered with Siefken, who early on could not command the strike zone. Barry Ducatte walked and was sacrificed to second base by Bates, then scored on consecutive singles by Dave Arends and Mike Maddie. Arends came home on Brooks Tunac's groundout to make it 2-0. Again, the Maples were facing a deficit.

But in the bottom half of the inning, Bates would battle his own nerves as Siefken, Glandt and Kauth walked. That brought up Rob Kaye, and his fielder's choice scored Siefken. Jeff Milius was up next, and he belted a fly ball to Memorial Field's infamously-deep left field. At 387 feet from home plate to the pole, the ball was caught but Glandt scored easily to tie the game.

The game raced forward to the next-to-last inning in just 45 minutes because neither team had another chance to score until the top of the sixth, when Troy should have gone ahead. Brooks Tunac walked and Steve Vinson singled, sending Sackett to the mound to replace Siefken with Newton. After a strikeout, Newton plunked Mike Husson in the back to load the bases with one out. But the Colts badly botched a two-strike safety squeeze, and the Maples turned a double play to escape the threat.

Entering the bottom of the seventh, the game was still tied at 2.

"The difference here was we weren't trailing and the top of the order was coming up again," Sheckell said. "Against Lathrup and Rice, I wasn't ever sure we were going to win, but because we had beaten Troy twice in the SMA season, that was a game I never thought we would lose."

As if on cue, the Maples' rally started innocuously.

Newton shot a single into left field. Pulling a page from Clouser's playbook, Sackett had Siefken sacrifice Newton to second. That brought up Glandt, and for a third-straight game he delivered, launching a double to the gap in right center field. Siefken scored. The game was over. Another wild celebration. The tournament jinx was over.

"If there was one guy to save us that day, it was Siefken," Sheckell said. "We were exhausted on a couple of different fronts, from prom and the tension of the Rice game. Todd had a second gear, we needed it, and he found it until we found another way to rally."

Kimball athletic director Chuck Jones led the postgame award ceremony. Each Maple was handed a small trinket to celebrate the accomplishment, but the Hall of Fame basketball coach who won eight district titles at Kimball held back awarding the trophy for Sackett. There was one problem: the "Old Man" was nowhere to be found.

"I had gone back to the car with the bats and helmets, like I did after any game," Sackett said. "One of the kids came running up to me and said, 'Coach, they're calling for you on the field! You have to come back to take the trophy!'"

That Seaholm had won the district was remarkable enough, but how they had won was stunning. The enthusiasm was almost intoxicating — Royal Oak's *Tribune* even ran a story titled, "Root for the Maples" — but the psychological dynamic unfolding was even more intriguing. The more the games tightened, the more the Maples' resolve strengthened.

Class A baseball
Root for the Maples

By Jerry Mawhinney
Tribune Correspondent

ROYAL OAK — Two rallies in the bottom of the seventh inning have given the Birmingham Seaholm baseball team a spot in the Class A regionals.

Playing on the day after the school's senior prom, the Maples edged Birmingham Brother Rice 2-1 in the semifinals and Troy 3-2 in the championship game of the Class A district Saturday at Memorial Park.

Combined with Seaholm's 3-2 win over second-ranked Southfield-Lathrup in a pre-district game, the Maples have three straight seventh-inning wins to take into the regional at Grosse Pointe North.

In the championship game, Troy scored twice in the first inning on a walk, a single by Dave Arends, an RBI double by Mike Maddix and an RBI groundout by Brooks Timko

to Moscovic's fly ball.

In the fourth inning, Rice pitcher Jeff Calcaterra gave up singles to the first two batters and then struck out the side to leave them stranded on base.

Rice's Mike Timko made a great running catch in the sixth inning to again defuse a rally for Seaholm.

But the Maples came through in the seventh

Mike Carroll walked, advanced to second on Brett Russell's single and moved to third on Matt Newton's single that bounced off home plate.

Carroll scored on Todd Sicfken's single, the second straight hit that bounced high off the plate.

Russell had advanced to third by the time and scored the winning run on a long fly ball

Royal Oak's *Daily Tribune* was one of the first media outlets outside of Birmingham to recognize and report on the remarkable attributes surrounding the Maples' title run.

The next production day for the *Observer & Eccentric* was Monday, and the 42-point typeface on the front of the sports page said it all...

Marty Budner's iconic headline in the *Observer & Eccentric* — now known as *Hometown Life* — spawned a title that aptly labeled Seaholm's march through the 1988 state playoffs and still follows this team today.

| Troy | (13-11) 200 000 0 - 2 4 5 |
| Birmingham Seaholm | (18-5) 000 000 1 - 3 16 2 |

WP: Newton. LP: Bates. 2B: **TC** - None; **BS** – Glandt. RBI: **TC** - Maddie, Tunac; **BS** - Glandt, Kaye, Milius.

CHAPTER 15:

MATT NEWTON

Class of 1989, Birmingham Seaholm

ON MARCH 24, 2018, MATT NEWTON AND I SAT DOWN TO DISCUSS

the Miracle Maples of almost 30 years ago. It was a Friday afternoon. I wanted to ask him how it changed him, and how it helped make him into who he is now: an older, wiser version of the cocky kid from Birmingham. He wanted to talk, get back to work and because it was the end of the month, make one more sale.

After living in Birmingham most of his adult life, Newton calls Ann Arbor home, so we met at Sidetracks, a retro pub in Ypsilanti, Michigan's Depot Town neighborhood. For nearby Eastern Michigan University students, it's a bit of a hideout. Outside, it was miserable. Freezing rain hissed from above and sleet was collecting on windshields and newspaper boxes. Inside, the old saloon's heating system was forcing down hot, cooked air. This is the essence of Michigan's weary season. You're tired of the weather that has accompanied life since Thanksgiving but you have six more weeks before warmer breezes tickle your senses. You're weary.

He strode into the old saloon, his smile and outsized personality immediately filling the oversized, outdated dining room. We sat down in the back corner of the restaurant and I lobbed a first, easy question at Newton: "How did Miracle Maples change you?"

Newton came out of his shoes swinging.

"On the field, I was a cocky dick and I wore my heart on my sleeve," Newton said. "It happened after the loss to Kimball. Losing that game

157

the way I did probably helped me get the most out of my ability. I didn't have the talent of the other guys, and I knew I wasn't going to be drafted or offered a scholarship, so I decided I never wanted to feel that way again. My mental approach changed after that game. I decided I had to get every ounce out of my ability and be the emotional leader of the team."

The 9-8 loss to Kimball was Newton's only loss of 1988. Because he was the pitcher of record in almost every come-from-behind win in the state tournament, he won 11 games. Now, he marched past talking about losing and into what made him and the Maples champions.

"I started out as our third baseman, but I wasn't very good, and because I didn't throw exceptionally hard, I pitched sporadically," Newton said. "I got benched and it pissed me off. And Don Sackett wouldn't give me another chance. I was just stewing when he threw a jab at me in practice. It changed everything."

During an intersquad scrimmage Sackett chided him, saying, "Newt, here's your only chance to play — why don't you go pitch!" Taking the mound as angry as he's ever been, Newton threw with a rage.

"I didn't care who I hit or where I hit them. I was furious. Carroll was up first, and I wind up and fire — I'm worried it's going to hit the backstop — but it goes right down the middle, and Carroll whiffs. I'm like, 'Whoa, what did I just do?'"

None of his Maple teammates touched his get-angry-and-throw methodology that day. He'd never been taught the mechanics of pitching, but after about 10 minutes, Newton realized this was his role. By accident, Sackett had found kryptonite.

"I might have thrown three innings the first half of the year, but from that one practice I became a regular pitcher in the rotation," Newton said. "It worked so much it became my new M.O., and that's why Kimball and everyone else hated me. What they didn't know was it was all because I was so pissed at Sackett."

We were halfway through our conversation when the bar began to shake. Bells were ringing and through the windows, lights were flashing. Now we knew why they called it Sidetracks. Suddenly sound had feeling as a commuter train barreled past the 100-year-old building, mere feet from our seats.

While every conversation near us screeched to a halt, 'Newt' plowed forward.

He spoke of the competing forces from different directions and among different players that created the adhesion required to change Seaholm's dynamic. Chris Kauth was given the third base job, joining Kaye, Sheckell and Glandt in giving the Maples a solid infield. Newton, a weakness in the field, instead became a strength on the mound. Whereas almost every season at Seaholm failed to meet expectations, beating Southfield Lathrup changed expectations, making a state championship possible.

The rest of the season was magical, Newton describing it as, "like nothing I've ever experienced in my life."

In 1989, Newton applied to and was accepted at Indiana University. Then he graduated from Seaholm. And then he eloped with Seaholm classmate Melissa Labarge a few weeks later.

"There's so much more to tell but not enough time to tell it," Newton said. "Basically, it was set up by her mom. My parents didn't know about it. I was 18, she was 17 — the court required her mother to sign a permission document because of her age — and I just showed up in Troy on the day of the wedding."

So off Newton went to Bloomington, Indiana, married to a girl completing her senior year and trying to walk-on to the Hoosier baseball team. In the Big Ten, even highly-recruited athletes wait a year or sometimes two before receiving significant playing time. Newton, a walk-on, hadn't been heavily recruited by anyone.

"Dude, I was beyond raw when I showed up, because I didn't have any of the coaching these players had, and the coaches saw this immediately and red-shirted me," Newton said. "My parents had found out I was married and wanted me to get a divorce, which looking back I should have, but I wasn't getting a divorce. I quickly realized I was going to take three or four years for me to play at Indiana, and it wasn't a good place for a married guy, either."

So on the advice of a friend, Newton downsized sight unseen to pint-sized Principia College, a school he described as a, "high school-sized college." A Division III, Christian Science-based school on the Mississippi River in Elsah, Illinois, Newton became a legend here, even though you've likely never heard of this school. His accomplishments are largely banished to sports pages of the pre-Internet era or on clunky HTML pages that haven't been updated in two decades.

In 1990, Newton's first year, Principia's football team went winless, prompting *Sports Illustrated* to rate the school's program as the worst in the country in 1991. But thanks to a connection with quarterback Jordan Poznick, Newton began to amass big numbers during games and most importantly, wins. Principia won more games in school history in the four years Newton and Poznick ran up and down the field using the run-and-shoot offense.

In an era before college football's spread offense-turned-RPO-obsessed passing schemes, Newton caught 286 passes, good for 3,636 yards and 34 touchdowns. His career totals were then second across all divisions of college football only to Jerry Rice, a feat the *St. Louis Post-Dispatch* noted in a feature titled "Newton's Law" as Newton approached the D-III record. With three games left in his senior season, Newton didn't surpass Rice, but he only needed 18 catches to reach the top spot in Division III, then 268 catches.

On Nov. 15, 1993, *Sports Illustrated* changed their tune, adding 'Newt' to their weekly Faces In The Crowd feature:

———

"Newton, a senior wideout for Principia (Ill.)
College, became the Division III leader in
career receptions with 264 when he made 13
catches in a 35-29 loss to Earlham College.
He broke the 12-year-old record of 258 set
by Bill Stromberg of Johns Hopkins. Newton
holds the division mark for receptions per
game (12.3) over a single season."[20]

———

Newton broke Division III records for career receptions, career yards per game (110.2) and receptions per game (8.7), a mark that was fourth among all divisions. He took both the first and second spots for single season average receptions per game in 1992 (12.3) and 1993 (12) and was named All-American in both seasons. He was top five in three other receiving categories. He was nominated for the Mel Berger Award, the Division III equivalent to the Heisman Trophy. He had broken four NCAA Division III receiving records, ranked among Division III leaders in five other receiving categories and set 14 Principia records in receiving, scoring and touchdowns.

He told the *Post-Dispatch's* Kevin E. Boone he had dreams of playing in the NFL while admitting his 6-foot-1, 200-pound frame and 4.65 time in the 40-yard dash meant, "I'll have to be a possession guy."

———

20   Sports Illustrated. Faces In The Crowd. Nov. 15, 1993

The call he hoped for never came from the NFL, but he walked away satisfied: "I didn't want to look back and say I didn't give it my best shot," Newton said.

Newton played three other sports at 'Prin," tying for the SLIAC scoring title as a basketball player, ranking second in the nation for steals and setting a Division III record with 17 in one game. He started three games for the school's baseball team and also played golf. He hadn't been graduated six months when the school inducted Newton into their Hall of Fame.

Newton was accomplished, graduated and unemployed. In 1996, he was named baseball coach at Seaholm, the circumstances surrounding his hire best described as awkward. Greg Porter had resigned in the fall of 1995 to take an assistant coach position at Oakland University. Ron Hillier was named new coach, but a booster club meeting just two weeks into his tenure scared him off, and he resigned immediately.

So Seaholm turned to Newton, who had no head coaching experience. The cocky kid who set over a dozen college records and a handful of NCAA marks was now standing on the foul lines, leading Seaholm with his teammate, Cam Mueller.

"Cam would always remind me of Don's line about Clouser," Newton said. "It was pretty obvious Coach Sackett wanted us to hate Clouser and Kimball, and he did a good job of it. But being on the coaching side of the rivalry, I have a lot of respect for what coach Clouser was able to do at Kimball over his long career. I know he had respect for what we did at Seaholm."

After the 1997 season, Newton and Mueller left Seaholm and relocated on Seven Mile Road to coach football at University of Detroit-Jesuit High. For the next eight seasons, Newton coached in the Catholic League's top division. In 1999 and 2001, U-D Jesuit reached the Division 2 semifinal. The staff was dynamic; Merchant would leave U-D Jesuit for Chippewa Valley High School, and Oscar Olejniczak, the line coach, took a graduate assistant position at Michigan State. He later became associate head coach at Campbell University in North Carolina before coming home to become head coach at U-D Jesuit and now, Royal Oak Shrine.

Newton and Labarge divorced in 2003; she moved to Carmel, Indiana with the two daughters from their marriage, now 19 and 17 years old. Newton re-married to Katie Esler, and they have two daughters and live in Ann Arbor.

Principia dropped football in February of 2009. Just a handful of people remember "Newt" at the school today. He's no longer a player in high school or college athletics, trading cleats and clipboards for smartphones and software as a professional executive coach for Better Up, a San Francisco-based start-up. Handling the midwest territory for the company, he's the older, wiser version of 'Newt' who first played for, then coached at Seaholm. But his outsized personality, the confidence he carries and the way he commands a room are still omnipresent, attributes all borne during the Miracle Maples experience.

"There's some of the guy I was then in me — tamed a bit, I guess — but Miracle Maples was where my success was born," Newton says. "I don't know how my life would have turned out if it hadn't happened, but it did happen. I'm proud of it, and I think it's safe to say my life looks a lot different because of it."

CHAPTER 16:

WINNING A MARATHON:

THE REGIONAL

JUST TWO GAMES AND 14 INNINGS STOOD BETWEEN THE MAPLES

and a berth in the Class A Final Four. Standing into front of the Maples was a school it hadn't seen much in 30 years.

The regional consisted of four district winners: Seaholm, Detroit Western, East Detroit and Warren Mott. Just like in the district, when the Maples had to play No.2 Lathrup and a well-rested Brother Rice team awaited, Seaholm had drawn the short end of the stick.

Seaholm drew East Detroit while Mott had drawn Western. Across the city of Detroit, AAU basketball had long ago replaced Little League baseball as the popular sport of choice. Because the city's schools had fewer baseball players to pick from, they attracted less-talented players. By the 1980s, PSL schools were ill-equipped to defeat the more skilled programs in the suburbs. The Cowboys reached the regional by mercying Detroit Southwestern and Detroit Kettering, 16-4 and 17-3, in the district, but Mott easily defeated the Public School League champions, 8-1.

Warren Mott and East Detroit both represented gritty, blue-collar enclaves within metro Detroit; in Seaholm they saw rich kids about to be punched in the mouth. What they didn't know was these Maples would be more than happy to punch back.

The regional took place at Grosse Pointe North. Like Birmingham, Grosse Pointe is one of Detroit's blue blood communities. Old money, as they say on the street or at the water cooler. It sits in Wayne County and borders Detroit but stately mansions line the city's more visible, majestic shoreline along Lake St. Clair.

First up was East Detroit, co-champions of the Eastern Michigan League. The Shamrocks defeated Grosse Pointe North, 6-0, in the district semifinal before stomping Warren Lincoln, 9-1, in the final.

Like Royal Oak, East Detroit is of a small, prideful city, comprised of saltbox homes, some sided in brick and others in aluminum, with side doors and stand-alone garages. Although the name implies otherwise, the city sits outside Detroit's eastern border. By the 1980s, almost every city in the tri-county area was trying to disassociate with the Motor City, and none tried harder than the Pointes and East Detroit. In 1992, East Detroit amended the city charter to rename itself Eastpointe, even though it held next to nothing in common with the stately Pointes. The school, however, is separate from the city and would hold out another 25 years until it renamed itself Eastpointe High School in 2017.

"The great irony is everyone is trying to claim ownership of Detroit and its' comeback," says Paul Nucci, a 1988 graduate of the school and former resident of the city, "and today it's no longer East Detroit."

This game would be a testosterone-fueled, roller-coaster affair, just the way the Maples liked it.

———

June 11, 1988; Grosse Pointe

North High School

Regional Semifinal No. 2: East

Detroit v. Birmingham Seaholm

———

For the fourth consecutive game, Seaholm was the home team. Newton started for the Maples, Phil VanAssche went for the Shamrocks. After setting down East Detroit in the first, Seaholm threatened when Siefken and Glandt led off and reached second and third, but Kauth and Kaye struck out swinging, and Milius grounded out to the shortstop. In the second, Newton fanned the side. When the Maples took the lead in their turn at bat, Carroll led off with a walk and scored on Sheckell's double.

East Detroit tied it up on Jimmy Lutzky's double in the third, and took the lead when Carroll's throwing error allowed Lutzky to score. The Maples tied it at two when Milius opened the fourth with a double, scoring on Cam Mueller's sacrifice fly to centerfield. After taking a 3-2 lead in the fifth, the Shamrocks exploded with three runs in the sixth. Kauth and Sheckell made back-to-back errors to put two on. A fielder's choice gave Newton a second out and a chance to escape the inning unscathed, but Sean Sacca scorched Newton for a three-run home run over the wall in leftfield.

East Detroit led 6-2, and Carroll could only watch in disbelief as the Shamrocks oozed emotion. The game was blown open. With just six outs left, Seaholm trailed by four. The magic seemed lost, and the miracle that occurred a weekend ago felt like a distant memory.

The Shamrocks' Rich Zoharanski (left) taunts the Maples after Sean Sacca (No. 44) hit a 3-run homer to put East Detroit up, 6-2, in the top of the sixth inning of the regional semifinal... *Photo by Dan Dean (Hometown Life)*

Carroll stepped in the batter's box to lead off the sixth inning. As he had done in the first inning, and as he did against Brother Rice, he triggered another rally by slapping a sharp single into the outfield grass. Sheckell and Mueller each walked to load the bases. It had almost become customary, a new set of heroes emerging game after game. Now it was Siefken's turn to save Seaholm.

Down four, Siefken swung with vicious force, the ball rocketing off his bat towards the deep reaches of the outfield. It shook everyone's senses, the same way a crack of thunder can shake you out of a deep sleep. As Sackett watched from the third base box, he said out loud, "Go... Go! GO!" On the bench, the Maples jumped to their feet, watching the ball soar until it easily cleared the cyclone fence, then exploding in cheers. With one swing, the game was tied! Now it was East Detroit's turn to watch Seaholm celebrate. Matt Newton was now pointing his finger at Rich Zahoranski and the rest of the Shamrocks: *"Right back at you bitches!"*

...but in the bottom of the 6th inning, Todd Siefken's grand slam tied the game at 6, Matt Newton returned the favor to East Detroit's bench. *Photo by Dan Dean (Hometown Life)*

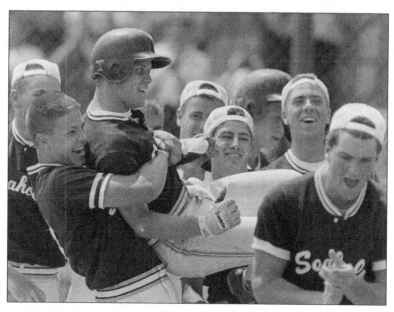

Matt Newton bearhugs Todd Siefken after his grand slam in the sixth inning against East Detroit. Jay Tauber, Rob Kaye and Jon Lanesky lead the celebration to the right. *Photo by Dan Dean (Hometown Life)*

Their opponents loathed it, but Seaholm fed off this hubris. This kind of bravado got the Maples this far, and it wasn't about to end anytime soon, either.

East Detroit didn't roll over. In the top of the seventh, the Shamrocks got back-to-back singles from Bob Martin and Ernie Townsley. In response, Newton rose to the occasion, striking out VanAssche and Zahoranski before getting Fred Julio to ground out to first unassisted.

Carroll singled in the seventh, but the Maples couldn't move him past second. The game went into extra innings. Again, the Shamrocks nearly took the lead again in the top of the eighth. After the first two hitters went down uneventfully, Sacca singled and went to third on Martin's double. Townsley's walk loaded the bases but Newton survived by getting VanAssche on a 1-3 groundout.

Again, phew.

After two uneventful half-innings, Seaholm came to bat in the bottom of the ninth, and just as it had happened against Lathrup, Brother Rice and Troy, an innocuous series of plays triggered the game-winning rally. Kauth grounded out to third. Kaye singled, and moved to second on a single by Milius. And in the on-deck circle stood Carroll.

Watching this unfold from the far depths of the left field corner was Carroll's father, Bob. He was easy to spot. He'd superstitiously worn the same maize-colored sweater to each of Seaholm's tournament games because the Maples hadn't lost since he started wearing the ugly good-luck charm during games in May. Now it was mid-June, and matter how hot it was, he wore the garment faithfully. He liked to smoke an occasional cigar, too, so he was often found down the foul line closest to Seaholm's dugout near one of the poles, the thick, black smoke encircling him.

While his son tried to author another storybook finish, the father stood nervously, shifting his weight back and forth, stopping only to puff on his stogie. On the fourth pitch of the at-bat, Carroll was sawed off by a fastball, his late swing sending a two-hopper towards Julio at second base. Milius broke immediately, passing in front of the ball, while shortstop Mike White was calling for the throw. Julio threw to White, who touched and shuffled off the bag before firing to first as hard as he could.

East Detroit was trying to turn the double play as Sackett threw up the stop sign. Just steps in front of third base, Kaye had no intention of obeying the signal.

"I'm going to try to score," Kaye said to himself, *"and if they fuck it up, we win."*

As the relay throw arrived at first base, a pregnant pause interrupted the shrill of the crowd watching the conclusion of the play. Everyone heard the 'thwack' of the ball into Townsley's glove and to most in the ballpark, they saw the throw beat Carroll, who dove head-first into the bag. But the umpire, who had rotated down from second towards first, screamed, "SAFE!"

It's the kind of call every umpire fears: a play that forces you to trade distance for angle because the play goes to multiple places faster than you can get there. The rationale behind all umpire positioning is simple: the closer a runner gets to home plate, the more important a potential call becomes. The problem with this play is the most important call is on the backend of the play at first base while the potential winning run is churning towards the plate.

The base umpire is moving has to see the clean catch of the ball, a tag of the bag and a transfer of the ball before pivoting towards first base to lock back into position to call the backend of the play. It's an amazingly quick sequence of events in just a few seconds.

When the call went against the Shamrocks, the arguing started immediately. Townsley lurched off the bag towards the umpire before realizing Kaye was roaring towards the plate. While others were screaming, Townsley turned and fired the ball towards catcher Ken Stacherski.

"I remember seeing Rob Kaye glance up and see there was a problem with the call at first," Sackett said. "He never hesitated; he was thundering towards the plate."

Townsley's slight inertia was all the advantage Kaye needed. He was already across the plate when Stacherski put down a tag, before shooting his mitt upward with the ball, hoping his action would successfully sell an out call. But when he looked up, the umpire's hands were already extending outward, a plume of dust rising upward around them.

Rob Kaye's desparate dash home included a head-first slide to avoid sliding into a tag by East Detroit's Ken Stacherski. *Photo by Dan Dean (Hometown Life)*

Rob Kaye turned over in celebration after realizing his improbable gamble to try to score on a fielder's choice advanced the Maples into the Class A regional final. *Photo by Dan Dean (Hometown Life)*

Chris Kauth (13) was the first to reach Rob Kaye as the Maples poured out of the dugout after defeating East Detroit, 7-6, in the final turn at bat in the bottom of the ninth inning at Grosse Pointe North. *Photo by Dan Dean (Hometown Life)*

The Maples were coming out of the dugout like a hockey team pours over the boards after a game-winning goal. Again. Seaholm wins. Again. Oh my God… Seaholm wins!

This fourth consecutive walk-off win — taking place on a most improbable 4-6-3-2 fielder's choice — was a delicious mix of resolve, moxie and fortune converging as their opponent's luck ran out. East Detroit hardly slinked away, their dejection understandable and emotion raw. A healthy amount of screaming from players, coaches and fans was directed at the umpires for several minutes.

"East Detroit had a bunch of tough kids, and I was afraid for the umpire after the game," Sackett said.

In their eyes, Seaholm hadn't won; East Detroit lost because an umpire's call allowed the game-winning run to score.

"That call… It still bothers me 30 years later," Jimmy Lutzky said. "It's tough because there's a part of us that knows if that call goes our way, if we win that game, we're just as capable of going to the state final and winning it."

It's also entirely possible the umpire called the play correctly. Sometimes, in the middle of an emotional microburst, players, coaches and fans see what they want to see as much as what actually happens. But the call isn't what lost the game for East Detroit. They lost because they were up 6-2 with six outs to go and couldn't close the door. They lost because they failed to score the potential go-ahead run with runners in scoring position after blowing the lead. That Seaholm won the game on a fielder's choice only obscured their failure to put the game out of reach.

Some coaches would be upset at their player for defying them in the moment, but Seaholm was running out of pitching and the game was headed for a 10th inning. Kaye's decision put the Maples to the regional final and Sackett wouldn't allow pride to get in the way of the moment, another subtle example of how the "Old Man" had changed his ways.

"I used to joke with the parents a lot, so I walked over as everyone was eating pizza and said, 'That was a helluva call I made, huh?' but no one laughed, because they weren't sure if I had waved him home or not," Sackett said. "What they knew is we won, we were going to play in the regional final and the season continued. That's what was important."

East Detroit	(17-8)	001	113	000	-	6	13	1
Birmingham Seaholm	(19-5)	110	104	001	-	7	11	4

WP: Newton. LP: VanAssche. 2B: **ED** – Martin, Lutzky; **BS** – Sheckell, Milius. HR: **ED** – Sacca; **BS** – Siefken. RBI: **ED** – Sacca 4, Lutzky, Zahoranski; **BS** – Siefken 4, Mueller, Sheckell, Carroll.

––––––

June 4, 1988; Grosse Pointe North High School

Regional championship: Warren Mott v. Birmingham Seaholm

––––––

If winning the district was exhilarating, the nine-inning regional semifinal was exhausting, a grind on Seaholm's talent and emotions. Next up was Warren Mott, champions of the Macomb-Oakland Athletic Conference (MOAC). With a berth in the state finals at stake, the Marauders were well-rested, and it was well past six o'clock before the the first pitch of the final was thrown.

Mott pounced on the Maples early, putting a pair of runs up in the bottom of the first. Seaholm rallied to tie in the top of the third, then hung another three on the board in the fourth inning. When that inning ended, umpires stepped in and halted the game. Too dark to continue today, they declared. The game would resume on the following Monday at 4 o'clock. Leading 5-2 and just 12 outs away from the school's first trip to the state finals, the game was in the bag in the minds of some of the Maples.

Don Sackett knew better. Sensing his team was overconfident, he shared his concern with Budner before everyone left the field.

"This works more to Mott's advantage. They'll be able to come back with their best pitcher," Sackett said. "I think it makes it tough on us."[21]

Undeterred, a handful of Maples decided it was time to announce their grand plan to the Birmingham community at large. On the morning of June 12, awaiting drivers on the Kensington Street train bridge was "State Champs" scrawled in crude, block letters from a spray paint can.

"Yeah, I was one of the instigators of that prank, although I can't remember if I was holding ankles or not," Siefken admitted. "Call it a premonition. Or stupidity. To say we were going to be state champs before we even made it out to East Lansing was a little much on our part. We were riding the wave."

The only problem was Seaholm still had to win the regional final, a state semifinal and the state final to make that statement come true.

Oops.

But to these Maples, their bravado and raw talent had carried them past Southfield Lathrup and Brother Rice. No school could be tougher than those two, right?

Wrong. On Monday, Sackett's statement from Saturday evening was printed in the *Observer & Eccentric.* When the game resumed, it was obvious Sackett was correct. A two-run home run by Dan Taylor and a steal of home by Jeff Piarchalski tied the score at five. In the fifth, Pete Moceri's home run put the Marauders up, 6-5.

---

21   Marty Budner, "On hold," Observer & Eccentric, June 13, 1988.

Seaholm had reached their final turn at bat, and they were flailing at the plate. After Kaye and Milius both hit into easy groundouts, the "state champs" were down to their last out. With the pressure of saving the season, who else but Carroll stepped up. He quickly fell behind 0-2 but battled, fouling off a handful of pitches and forcing a handful of misses. Finally, the count was 3-2, and then, ball four. Carroll had passed the torch.

"That was the at-bat of the season," Sheckell said. "The game was pretty much over and again, we found a way."

Up next was Sheckell, and facing a pitcher in the stretch, he also walked. With Carroll moving up to second base, Sackett sent Newton in as a pinch runner. Mueller was up next and like Carroll, he fell behind 0-2. Down to their last strike for the second time, and with Newton getting as far off second base as he could, Mueller lined the next pitch into the outfield. Because there were two outs, Newton was moving the instant bat met ball and he glided home with the tying run, his hands in the air while his teammates screamed their approval from the bench.

From left to right, Crede Colgan, Jeff Lanesky, Mike Carroll, Jeff Milius, Jay Tauber, Rob Kaye and Todd Glandt watch anxiously as another improbable miracle unfolds in the top of the seventh against Warren Mott. Seaholm won the game, 13-10, in eight innings to punch their ticket to the state finals. *Photo by Dan Dean (Hometown Life)*

Cam Meuller delivered the game-tying single to score Matt Newton, whose bravado and enthusiasm cannot be contained while resuscitating the Maples' miracle run to the state title. Celebrating behind him is trainer Bill Watson, Bill Stephenson, Crede Colgan, Todd Glandt, Mike Carroll and Jeff Milius. *Photo by Dan Dean (Hometown Life)*

The game saved, Newton retired the side to send the game to extra innings. That's when Seaholm exploded.

Siefken walked, and Glandt blasted a double to put the Maples up, 7-6. Kauth walked. Kaye singled. Milius doubled. Carroll walked and Sheckell singled. Mueller singled again. The Maples were circling the bases. It would take 22 minutes and 12 hitters before to retire the side. The Maples were up, 13-6, and only a major implosion could prevent a trip to the state finals now.

And that's when Seaholm almost gave it all back. Kauth walked the first two hitters, then struck out the No. 9 hitter in the lineup. After a single scored a run, Kauth notched his second strikeout. But two more singles sandwiched a walk, and with four runs in, the tying run was at the plate and the winning run standing in the on-deck circle, Sackett had seen enough. Milius replaced Kauth, and he fanned Mott's Paul Kaiser on three pitches to send Seaholm to their first state final in school history.

Winning the marathon had required a breathtaking effort spanning two games, three days and 17 innings. The Maples sent 91 hitters to the plate, pounded out 20 runs, 24 hits and still, they found themselves down to their last strike in two different situations. Now five games into the state tournament, they had scored the winning run in their last turn at bat five straight times. In three of those games, they trailed entering the last inning; twice they were being shut out when they rallied to win.

Besides Carroll, the M&M boys — Milius and Mueller — were heroes against Mott. Milius knocked in the game-tying run and slammed the door to earn the save, while Mueller had five hits in as many trips, knocked in two and scored twice. Like Carroll, Glandt was emerging as a daily hero, having batted in four with his double and a home run from the previous day.

The dramatic way in which the Maples continued to advance was now a breathtaking drama, attracting attention from Royal Oak's *Daily Tribune* along with Budner at the *Observer & Eccentric*.

Seaholm's unlikely march through the Class A playoffs was noticed by newspapers outside of the Maples' coverage zone, such as Royal Oak's *Daily Tribune*.

"Statistically speaking, what is the probability of winning five games in your final at-bat?" Sheckell asks, still marveling at the improbability. "In the regional, both games took forever, they were both emotional, high-scoring games, and the second game was suspended due to darkness. We had to come back on Monday to finish it. What are the odds of winning all of those scenarios? I can't even begin to calculate it."

The state's final four was set, and Seaholm was comfortably wearing Cinderella's slippers.

The Observer & Eccentric's front page following Seaholm's fifth-consecutive win in their final at-bat and 14th victory in a row captured the excitement of the Maples' rise to the Class A final four.

Birmingham Seaholm   (20-5) 002 300 17   - 13 13 2
Warren Mott   (18-5) 200 310 04   - 10   8 1

WP: Newton. LP: Moreci. SV: Milius. 2B: **WM** – None; **BS** – Glandt, Milius. HR: **WM** – Moceri, Petrovich, Taylor; **BS** – Glandt. RBI: **WM** – Petrovich 2, Taylor 2, Moreci, Piarchalski; **BS** – Glandt 4, Mueller 3, Russell 3, Kaye, Milius, Sheckell.

game suspended June 11 in the 4th inning due to darkness; resumed June 13.

CHAPTER 17:

BOTTOMS UP: THE STATE SEMIFINAL

ON JUNE 17, 1988, DON SACKETT DISCOVERED FOR HIMSELF

why the state finals was so intoxicating. School was out for the summer. Only one school-sponsored activity remained: his baseball team's trip to Michigan State.

Today, one might expect a climate-controlled charter bus with upholstered seats and video screens for a trip to the state finals, but 30 years ago, school districts still owned school buses. On the morning of the state semifinal, a yellow bus with "Birmingham Public Schools" stenciled on both sides pulled into the back parking lot of the school at 8:30. The Maples filed onto the bus and threw their equipment bags into open benches as the bus lurched forward, the familiar rumble from the rear exhaust kick-starting the two-hour trek towards East Lansing.

Taylor Kennedy and East Kentwood played the first semifinal at 10 a.m. Sackett had the team leaving at 8:30 to get there in time to see some of Kennedy and East Kentwood. Steve Avery, 12-0 with a 0.34 ERA, would start for Kennedy. He had been picked third overall by the Atlanta Braves three weeks earlier in the amateur draft. More than a few teams had been skittish about drafting Avery because, having signed a full scholarship to attend Stanford, he had some contract leverage in hand.[22]

The games he pitched were an event, even among umpires. Rich Fetchiet made his name as a college umpire in Michigan, working the plate in the 1999 NCAA Division I final before becoming the assignor

---

22   Ken Rosenthal, "Orioles Didn't Want to Draft Steve Avery," *Baltimore Sun*, October 19, 1991, retrieved from http://www.articles.latimes.com.

for the Big 10, the Big 12, the Mid-American Conference and several smaller leagues. He's known nationally within the college baseball community as "Fetch" but in the 1980s, he was still working a healthy bit of high school baseball. For an important game like a regional final, it was no surprise to see Fetchiet on the plate the day Avery fanned 17 of the 21 hitters he retired. Oh, he also hit two home runs.

"He was an outstanding outfielder who could hit, so he was the best player on the field whenever and wherever he played," Fetchiet said. "But when he pitched, he could throw four pitches for strikes and had a poise that overmatched hitters mentally and physically. His stuff was electric."

On the belief Avery would be available to pitch at least a few innings in a state final game, Sackett felt it was important for his team to get a look at this future major leaguer.

"Watching Avery was the first time we had ever seen that kind of talent up close, and he looked like a pitcher should: tall, slender, and the way he threw the ball compared to me, Newton or anyone else we had seen was totally different," Siefken said. "We saw the velocity on his pitches, the way he performed...it was impressive."

When the Maples arrived, Kennedy led, 2-0, on a pair of first innings runs. East Kentwood rallied to tie the game with two runs in the fifth. In the sixth they should have taken the lead. The lead-off hitter touched Avery for a single before stealing second base. Avery was called for a balk, moving the go-ahead run just 90 feet from home with no one out, but he roared back to strike the next two hitters out before inducing a ground out to wiggle off the hook.

Mark Wortman took over for East Kentwood in the fifth for and he matched Avery pitch for pitch through the ninth inning. In the top of the 10th, Avery retired the side and as he walked back the dugout, Sackett smiled. By pitching 10 full innings and reaching the 30-out limit, Avery was ineligible to pitch in tomorrow's championship game if Kennedy could survive.

In a matter of a few pitches, that became reality. East Kentwood brought in a new pitcher in the bottom of the 10th inning. Chris Bronis singled, moved up on a sacrifice and came home a few pitches later on Mike Giacamontonio's double. Kennedy, the highest-ranked team left in the Class A bracket, had advanced.

Next up was Seaholm and Port Huron, two schools fighting to wear the same set of slippers. On paper, the Big Reds appeared formidable. They were co-champions of the Eastern Michigan League with Anchor Bay and East Detroit — no one had to remind the Maples how tough the regional semifinal had been — while winning Port Huron's first-ever district and regional titles. Meanwhile, Seaholm finished three games out of first in the SMA and had needed magic in the last turn at bat in five straight games to reach the semifinal.

At some point, the averages say the magic runs out, but in those five games, the Maples defeated three league champions. They didn't win their league, but the SMA was as tough as any other conference in the state, evidenced by three SMA teams reaching a district final. Thanks to an extraordinary set of circumstances, Seaholm on the doorstep of the state final. Could the Maples continue to flourish without the underdog mentality that had rallied them through the first five tournament games?

———

June 17, 1988; Kobs Field at

Michigan State University

Class A semifinal No. 2: Port Huron

v. Birmingham Seaholm

———

Sackett hadn't been overly worried about the semifinal, but that changed within a few minutes when Newton loaded in the top of the first. After retiring the first two hitters, a walk to catcher Jeff Daniels was the innocuous trigger. Tom Wilson followed with a single to right, and when Cam Mueller bobbled the ball, Daniels cruised into third.

Sackett watched from the dugout and thought, *"It's taken me a quarter-century to get here and we're going to play like the Bad News Bears?"*

So Sackett ordered Newton to intentionally walk the left fielder, Tom Jokie, a decision that carried the risk of accelerating the inning. This was the kind of decision-making Sackett had largely avoided throughout the playoffs, but Newton made the gamble pay off by inducing Jim Feher to ground out on a sidearm curveball.

In the bottom half of the inning, Glandt reached when Port Huron first baseman Jim Fournier caught a ground ball but threw errantly behind Trevor Lawson covering the base. It was the first of four Port Huron errors. With two outs, Kaye walked. That brought Milius to the plate, and he blasted a 2-2 pitch over the head of Wilson in centerfield. Glandt and Kaye, best friends off the field, raced around to score, and in a matter of minutes, Seaholm had gone from a likely deficit to a two-run lead. The momentum swing had the Maples roaring on the bench.

In the fourth, Kaye led off with a double. He would be picked off, but walks to Milius, Carroll, Sheckell and Mueller made it 3-0. Lawson entered the semifinal with a 1.73 ERA and 120 strikeouts on the season,[23] but now Port Huron coach Dick Hillaker pulled his infielders to the lip of the grass, trying to cut down the lead run at the plate instead of letting his pitcher try to work past the lower third of the lineup.

His decision to risk making the inning bigger was understandable: the Big Reds had managed just a single and walk since the first inning.

---

23   Jim Whymer, "Big Reds lose in semifinal," *Port Huron Times Herald,* June 18, 1988.

Running out of turns at bat, Hillaker knew the Big Reds couldn't allow any more runs.

But just as Lawson went into his delivery, Hillaker had second thoughts and barked at his middle infielders to back-peddle into double play depth. Russell rapped a ground ball at James, and the evolving distance created a short hop that James misplayed. As it skipped awkwardly past his glove and into the outfield, two more runs scored to put a dagger in Port Huron. It was 5-0 and the game was effectively over.

A hit batsman, a balk and four more hits scored two more runs for the Maples in the sixth, as Seaholm took the semifinal with ease, 7-2. Newton went the distance and allowed just two hits and no earned runs. The two Big Red runs came courtesy two errors, three walks and five wild pitches in the last two turns at bat. After the game, Hillaker shared his frustration with Jim Whymer, sports editor of the *Port Huron Times Herald*.

"I didn't think (Newton) threw very well in the regional and I still don't know if he's any good … but he must be because he stopped us pretty good. You have to give the kid credit. He did the job today."[24]

Sought by the gaggle of reporters covering the finals, Newton delivered another healthy dose of bravado, telling reporters the Maples were disappointed they wouldn't be able to face Avery.

"We kind of wanted to face him. I've read a lot about him and we thought we could hit him," Newton said as reported by Chris Gerbasi of the *Oakland Press*, "but now we'll go against their second-best and we'll take whatever we get."[25]

Sackett listened to this and laughed out loud, thinking to himself, *"Son, you don't want any of that medicine. Be thankful you don't have to take it."*

---

24   Jim Whymer, "Big Reds lose in semifinal," *Port Huron Times Herald*. June 18 1988.
25   Chris Gerbasi, "Seaholm Earns Trip to Class A Final," *Oakland Press*, June 18, 1988.

Port Huron	(21-7) 000 001	1	-	2	2	4
Birmingham Seaholm	(21-5) 200 302	x	-	7	11	3

WP: Newton. LP: Lawson. 2B: **PH** – None; **BS** – Kaye. 3B: **BS** — Milius. RBI: **PH** – None. **BS** – Milius 2, Kaye, Mueller.

Late afternoon turned to evening. The sun was setting slowly and the metaphor of the moment was unmistakable. It had taken 25 years, but in the twilight of his coaching career, he'd finally made it to the head of the night before the biggest game of the season. Just as exciting as reaching the state final was the fact Seaholm wouldn't have to face Avery. The Maples had a real chance to steal the Class A crown.

Taking time to enjoy a small indulgence, Sackett sat down to dinner at the Sheraton Hotel with a wink to his better half, Wilma. The moment was beyond sweet; he hadn't enjoyed a baseball season this much since the two of them were college sweethearts at Michigan State in the late 1950s.

A handful of Oakland County coaches had already occupied the chair Sackett sat in that night. Chuck Mikulas took Hazel Park to the championship game in 1974. Clarkston's Paul Tungate won the Class A title in 1976. Larry Reichle won it all with West Bloomfield in 1983. Chuck Apap's Walled Lake Western squad won it all in 1984. And no one had to remind Sackett about Clouser's four appearances in the title game.

The last time Sackett stepped between the lines here, he'd been a Spartan. The success he enjoyed as a workman-like performer at Michigan State had eluded Sackett at Seaholm, but this was a just dessert for all the years he toiled fruitlessly. The night's dinner was served. As he reached for his utensils he noticed Carroll approaching the table, walking with an urgency a parent immediately recognizes. But even Sackett didn't realize the gravity of the situation when he turned and asked, "What's up, Mike?"

"Coach, Siefken's drinking in his room."

Just like that, the moment was over. Siefken was Seaholm's best pitcher. He was supposed to start the championship game in a little more than 12 hours. But right now, he was pounding down beers with some buddies in a hotel room paid for by the Birmingham school system.

Seaholm's teachers and coaches were well-schooled in these kind of situations. Around Michigan, Seaholm students are derisively called "Birmingham Brats," a not-so-subtle title for the affluence these young adults are surrounded by. Wet goods pried from a parent's liquor cabinet? Seen that. Designer drugs? Been there. Grabbing the keys to Dad's sports car or playing loose and fast in a house pool while unsuspecting parents worked miles away? Not unheard of. Many students wore designer labels and came from households with six-figure incomes.

Many Seaholm students had come up to East Lansing for the semifinal. Word of the semifinal win traveled back to Birmingham from hotel rooms or payphones, a reminder of how our society communicated in the prehistoric age before SmartPhones and SnapChat. Siefken's friends, with a case of beer already in hand, decided it was as good a time as any to start the party.

Carroll, one of Siefken's best friends, was doing exactly what was asked of him as a captain. Carroll had become the standard bearer, the blow-up from a year ago aside, because he was always the first one on the practice field and the last one to leave. But with this team, nothing good seemed to happen without a little drama, so Carroll and Sackett, combatants a year earlier were now teammates in tackling this incident.

"Jesus Christ..." Sackett said, pushing himself away from the table, "... let's get up there." In his head, the whispers were already starting. *"Please don't let this happen to me now..."* But it was happening, and the possibility of one his players soaked in alcohol the night before the big game was filling his head faster than he could cover the walk to the elevator.

The doors to the car opened, the pair stepped in and they rose. As the doors re-opened, Carroll told his coach he didn't know who brought the booze. Now walking down the hall, Sackett asked how drunk Siefken was. Carroll began to answer: "I don't know, but he's probably…" and Sackett decided he no longer wanted to know the answer, cutting him off by saying, "Let's see how bad it is first."

Sackett would not broach the topic of eliminating his best pitcher from pitching tomorrow's game too soon. As they approached the room, there was no loud music but Sackett banged on the door the same way police officers knock on doors when they serve an arrest warrant. A few shadows flashed past the peephole before the door opened slowly. Siefken was sitting on the ledge by the window, playing it cool in front of his friends.

"Hey Coach…what's up?"

Siefken's friends stood in stunned silence as the room's temperature plummeted from the icy glare on the faces of Sackett and Carroll unmistakable.

Sackett needed just one angry question to sum up the moment: "Todd, what the hell are you doing?!!"

Siefken stood frozen, the gears in his head grinding with the self-revelation he had jeopardized this potential jewel for his coach and his teammates. His friends, now fully aware of their role as accomplices, were shamed, too. Sackett was seething, but he was mustering every option possible to keep his best pitcher eligible and his team's miracle alive, too.

First, he focused on Siefken's friends and barked, "Get the hell out of this room. Grab your shit and get out!"

While Siefken's friends hustled out of the room, Sackett gave serious consideration to Saturday. He felt like a state trooper making a traffic stop — and the questions swirled inside his head: *"Did we interrupt the drinking before it truly started? Can he still pitch tomorrow?"*

Sackett had tired long ago of reading the same predictions and watching the same schools succeed year after year. Finally, Seaholm advances to a state title game and it's being called a miracle. But miracle or not, Sackett was going to consider every option to keep it alive. Allowing Siefken to play was a risk he was willing to take. Carroll was already two steps ahead of his coach, immediately recognizing what was at stake for his coach and his school.

"We can get him some water and coffee, and we'll see how he is in the morning," Carroll asserted calmly. "Will that do, coach?"

Sackett replied: "We'll come up here in the morning, just you and I. We'll make a decision then, okay?"

It would never pass muster today, a 56-year-old coach and an 18-year-old captain making the conscious decision to keep a drinking incident under their hats, but Sackett and Carroll were Seaholm's odd couple. They were way past weird. Beyond the big blowup between them, the two worked well together. Carroll had been given a second chance, and this was an opportunity to pay his coach back.

As a captain, he spared Siefken in part because he knew what it was like to be on the outside looking in. But in a more narrow context, he knew this was a legacy game. For his coach. For his teammates. For Seaholm, and for Birmingham. Carroll was only interested in being his coach's loyal soldier.

"No problem, coach."

Sackett was no longer hungry. It was too late to eat, anyway. The Maples had reached the crossroads. In 12 short hours, they'd find out if the ride to and from the ball would end as a dream or a nightmare.

CHAPTER 19:

A WINNING STREAK ENDS: THE STATE FINAL

IN THE MORNING HOURS PRECEDING THE CLASS A CHAMPION-
ship game, Don Sackett didn't know who his starting pitcher would be,
but he knew who wouldn't be pitching.

"If this isn't a miracle, nothing is," Sackett thought.

In Kennedy's 10-inning, 3-2 win over East Kentwood, Avery didn't
just record outs, he dominated by fanning 19 of the 30 hitters he retired. Not having to face Michigan's Mr. Baseball, with his 13-0 record,
196 strikeouts and 0.39 ERA meant this would be Sackett's best and
only chance to grab the ring. It was just hours away from his grasp but
his long climb to the mountain top was hardly assured.

Besides having to figure out who was going to pitch, he had to find
a way to stop a team that won 16 straight games and was loaded with
enough talent to win the game without him.

After breakfast with Wilma, Sackett put on his uniform, then sat
down to fill out his lineup. He carefully plugged name after name in
each succeeding slot knowing the best player in the state wouldn't be
available to pitch. Siefken, if he could play, would lead off. Glandt,
Kauth and Kaye followed. Milius hit fifth, followed by Carroll and
Sheckell. Mueller and Russell rounded out the lineup. Sackett wouldn't
need to use a designated hitter; Siefken, hero of the regional final with
his timely grand slam, would hit for himself.

The lineup hadn't changed all season. There was no reason to start
tinkering with it now. It was time to leave. First pitch was scheduled

for 10 a.m. He stood, exhaled, and thought, *"Let's hope these jokers have enough in the tank to finish the job."*

Siefken remained noticeably absent as the Maples warmed up on Kobs Field at 9:30 a.m. At 9:40, Sackett put his emergency plan into motion. Milius, Seaholm's jack-of-all-trades and the hero of the semi-final the day before, was sent to the bullpen to warm up.

"I remember thinking, *"This is our starting pitcher for the state championship game?"* Sheckell said. "Even though I didn't run with that crowd, I knew Siefken was one of the guys who liked to party, so I'd heard a little bit about the night before, but when Milius started walking towards the bullpen, it grabbed everyone's attention."

It was a scene straight out of the movie *Bull Durham*, when Tim Robbins' character, Ebby Calvin "Nuke" LaLoosh, shows up late for his professional debut because he's fooling around with a local girl in the lockerroom. Like what happens in the movie, Siefken finally walks up to the field and Sackett gave him a healthy dose of stink eye. Then he sent him to warm up anyway. Milius went back to the outfield to take fly balls.

It looked like Seaholm was staggering into the title game. With these Maples, it was business as usual. Siefken was the best pitcher Seaholm had and no one questioned why he was starting the championship game.

"Newton had the better record, but Siefken was our best pitcher," Carroll said, "and he definitely pitched better a little hung over."

June 18, 1988; Kobs Field at Michigan State University

Class A championship: Birmingham Seaholm v. Taylor Kennedy

Kennedy (25-3) was the home team. The Eagles' Rob Mowery started for the Eagles, and Seaholm jumped all over him.

In the first inning, Siefken and Glandt led off with consecutive singles. Kauth hit into a fielder's choice, and Kaye was put out by the first baseman unassisted. With two outs, Milius pinged a seeing-eye single into left on an 0-2 count. Both runners scored to put the Maples up, 2-0.

In the third, Siefken tripled to lead off. Glandt walked, and Siefken scored on Kauth's sacrifice fly to centerfield. Kaye singled, moving Glandt to third. He scored on Milius' sacrifice fly. Carroll singled and Kaye came around to score. The Maples sent seven hitters to the plate and led, 5-2.

In the fourth, Seaholm sent eight to the plate. Mueller opened with a walk, and Russell followed with a single. Siefken was put out by the second baseman, but Glandt singled and Kauth hit a sacrifice fly. Kaye and Milius singled before Carroll flew out to right field to end the inning, but the Maples had chased Mowery from the hill. It was now 8-2, Seaholm.

After Kennedy came back with a pair of runs in the fifth, the assault continued in the sixth. Kauth led off with a double, followed by another Kaye single. Milius reached on an error, and Carroll hit a sacrifice fly to center field before Mueller singled. Another eight hitters to the plate, three hits and three more runs.

When Siefken walked out for the bottom of the sixth, it was 11-4. Pitching with a huge lead late in a tournament game, much less the biggest game of the season, was foreign territory for Seaholm. In the bottom of the sixth inning, that's when the problems started.

Siefken fanned the first hitter, but Joe Deliz belted a triple. Chris Donahey, Avery's best friend, singled to score Deliz. A few minutes later, Chris Bronis doubled to score Donahey and it was 11-6. Sackett decided to replace his ace with Newton, who had won all six games in the tournament. He gave up another run but got Seaholm back in the dugout with an 11-7 lead.

He was tired from pitching six innings the day before, but Newton thought he had one more good inning in him. Would it be enough to hold off Kennedy? The final inning started easily enough. Rob Kaye handled Mowery's ground ball to shortstop flawlessly, an easy play for the first out. The catcher, Stickney, singled and Ganzberger, the designated hitter, walked. Now Newtown uncorked a wild pitch. He got ahead of pinch hitter Mike Meade with two quick strikes but couldn't put him away. Meade's two-strike single scored both runners, making it 11-9.

The tying run was walking to the plate and the potential winning run was standing in the on-deck circle. Sackett asked for time. He trudged slowly to the mound. He didn't have a better option than Newton, so his slow, measured steps were buying his pitcher as much time as possible to rest. The irony was impossible to miss: the Maples were now the team desperate to hang on, and Kennedy was on the doorstep of a miracle of their own.

After winning five-straight games in their final at-bat, the tables were turned on the Maples in the state final. Seaholm had run weary on pitching and was fighting to hold off a miracle in the making at the hands of Taylor Kennedy. *Photo by Dan Dean (Hometown Life)*

Sackett shuffled slowly back to the dugout and the game continued with Donahey, who hit a fly ball to right field. Siefken clutched it. Two outs. That brought up Bronis, who hadn't made an out all day — a triple, double, two singles and three runs scored — as Avery and his .431 batting average awaited on deck. The count got to 2-2. Newton set and heaved, and Bronis lifted his offering high in the air towards left field. All Milius had to do was move a few feet. He waited for it to fall, then clutched it for the last out.

Avery walked back from the on-deck circle as Milius sprinted towards the middle of the diamond. His teammates, including everyone from the dugout, were already there. It had happened.

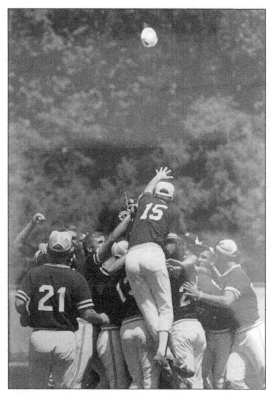

Seaholm's dog pile in the middle of the field after winning the Class A state final was genuine — anything but obligatory — as the Maples turned the most improbable run to the championship into a reality. *Photo by Dan Dean (Hometown Life)*

Speaking to reporters after the game, Newton said, "I told (my teammates) I'd get them out before Avery came up. I wasn't throwing as hard today (as against Port Huron)," he said, "but I still had confidence I could get them out."

Budner neatly summed up the Maples' bravado: "Newton epitomized Seaholm's state championship run — confident to the very end."

Winning seven straight games — coming back in five consecutive games before nearly being walked off in the state final — made up for 17 frustrating years of failing to advance past the district, mostly at the hands of Kimball.

"I always dreamed we would win the state championship in basketball. I never dreamed of winning the state championship in baseball," Sheckell says. "It shows you when you stick to it, compete all the time and never give in, anything can happen. We competed in every game, and all the tough, close games we had a chance to win, we won."

At Royal Oak's Red Run Golf Club, it wasn't yet late afternoon when someone stopped Clouser to tell him Seaholm won the state championship.

"I remember thinking to myself, "A lot of people are going to call this luck, but Seaholm's not the only team that's had some luck," Clouser said. "Remember, they were close enough to take advantage of some situations and win five straight ball games in the seventh inning or later. They took advantage of those situations when it mattered most and turned it into a state championship."

Less than a week later, Clouser managed the state's annual prep All-Star game at Tiger Stadium. Avery was his starting pitcher.

"That the Maples didn't have to have to face him for so much as an inning or an out was very lucky," Clouser said. "He was outstanding, and he was great for the Atlanta Braves for a long time."

But more than avoiding having to face Avery, the biggest break Seaholm received was the blind draw that created the finals bracket. By drawing Port Huron, Seaholm avoided two heavyweights, Taylor Kennedy and East Kentwood. When that semifinal went 10 innings, therefore making Avery unable to pitch, it was suddenly possible for Seaholm to do the impossible.

Amid the immediate aftermath of the victory, there was one piece of unfinished business between Carroll and Sackett. A day earlier, Country Day coach Frank Orlando found Carroll after the Yellow Jackets lost the semifinal and told him, "We win the state title if you're our catcher."

Now Sackett found Carroll in the middle of Kobs Field and cemented the stakes of a friendship that endures today.

"Mike, we don't win this title without you," Sackett said. "I just want you to know I'm glad you came back, and I'm glad this happened for you."

It really had happened. For all of them.

State champion Maples have many heroes

The improbability wining 16 straight games en route to a state title was dissected in articles like this one from the *Observer & Eccentric in* the weeks and months to follow, ultimately never forgotten by those who witnessed it happen.

Birmingham Seaholm   (22-5)   203   303   0   -   11   16   1

Taylor Kennedy   (25-4)   110   023   2   -   9   13   2

WP: Siefken. LP: Mowery. SV: Newton. 2B: **BS** – Kauth; **TK** – Bronis. 3B: **BS** – Kaye, Siefken; **TK** – Bronis, Deliz. RBI: **BS** – Milius 4, Carroll 2, Kauth 2, Kaye, Mueller; **TK** – Deliz 2, Avery, Bronis, Donahey, Giacomantonio, Mowery.

CHAPTER 18:

TODD SIEFKEN

Class of 1988, Birmingham Seaholm

ON THE GREY, NONDESCRIPT DAY THE MIRACLE MAPLES RE-

turned to Birmingham Seaholm to celebrate the 30-year anniversary of the 1988 championship, Todd Siefken, the Maples' best pitcher that season, was nowhere to be found.

After being honored between games of a doubleheader, many of the 1988 Maples went to a house party hosted by Rob Kaye. At 9:30 p.m., the door opened and Don Sackett's reaction grabbed everyone's attention.

"Of course! Look who shows up late!"

Siefken missed the baseball game at Seaholm because his flight from Colorado was delayed. Now 30 years later Siefken once again showed up to the big party late but made a grand entrance and pulled it off like a champion, too.

"It was amazing to watch the room explode when he walked in," Mark Sackett said of that night. "Siefken was never one to shy from making a big entrance. His face looked the same, although his hair was dark and a bit grey, but he has a presence and energy like no one else on that team."

Today, Siefken admits his outsized personality was a dichotomy of sorts. He was the prototypical wild child, his interest in playing sports and hanging out with friends far exceeding his desire to excel in the classroom. Growing up in a home within eyesight of Seaholm's athletic fields, he was chronically late to school and practice. But as Seaholm's quarterback in 1986-87, his talent and ability to perform was obvious to his peers. He was a member of the committee of students, parents and administrators pulled together to help the school hire Fraser in the winter of 1987.

"There's a stigma to being a pastor's kid, and I justified that stereo-type to a T," Siefken says. "I certainly got in my share of trouble, but my parents were always supportive, and they loved I was involved in athletics. Athletics and having a good time with my friends was more of an interest to me that schoolwork. Because of that, my parents held a pretty good leash, and sometimes I yanked on it as hard as I could."

Siefken is a executive general manager for Wyndham Vacation Rentals. Married to Jenny Siefken, the couple has a 10-year-old son, Liam and reside in Steamboat Springs, Co. He oversees over 20 properties and draws on the experience of Miracle Maples often within the context of his day-to-day responsibilities.

"You never give up. Even when you think there's no way out, you keep fighting. It might be luck, it might be skill, it might be a combination of both, but if you don't put yourself out there and give yourself a chance, you'll never know," Siefken said. "The 'Miracle Maples' experience taught me how to be a winner. You don't realize how little you know about winning until you've done it. In that context, I fall back on those experiences as an adult often."

There's another side of this experience, the cringe-worthy moments he draws on as a parent, specifically drinking beers with his buddies on the eve of the title game. It's fair to say his success could have easily been derailed in a matter of minutes, and there would be no moment to draw from in the aforementioned context of winning in life.

"It was a different time, and the level of tolerance in our society for this kind of behavior has been whittled down to nothing, as it should," Siefken admits. "If I was on the younger Todd Siefken's shoulder, trying to mentor him through the evening, I would tell him, 'You're an athlete. You need to think and act like an athlete. To be an athlete, you need to take care of yourself mentally, physically and spiritually.' The older version of me looks at partaking in this activity on the eve of the biggest game of my life up to that point and makes a different decision. I've got a 10-year-old, and if I were to coach and mentor him, the first lesson I teach him is, 'You've got to take care of yourself.'"

What also remains is a twinge of sadness for how and where his high school career ended, again thanks to a few moments of lapsed judgment.

"I missed the chance to raise my arms as a champion on the mound because I was running out of gas and had to be replaced in the championship game," Siefken said. "Instead, I had to do that from right field. I'm thankful that Coach Sackett allowed me to stay in the game, which meant I was still part of the team that was on the field when that last out was made, but I didn't get a chance to win it from the mound. I always look back and wonder, 'If I had not been drinking and got to bed early the night before, would I have had the extra 'Oomph!' the next day instead of Newton having to come in and finish it up?'"

We all make choices, and from those choices and consequences is how we learn life's lessons. You only learn after you've made the mistake, unless you learn not to make someone else's mistake. Looking back, Siefken realizes why being caught drinking before the championship game didn't sit well with his teammates.

"Winning those games the way we did was the reason we were there, and I put it all at risk," Siefken said. "We all these forces coming together at the same time, and a big part of it was all the different abilities and personalities that had come together. There was a perfect mix that allowed it come together: the motivator (Newton), the quiet power hitter (Glandt), the athlete who was precise and methodical (Sheckell), the guy who was reckless (Siefken). All the individuals made the formula work and I'm very thankful to have been a part of it."

EPILOGUE

SIMILAR TO WHEN I SAT DOWN TO PEN AN INTRODUCTION — A

task I smartly abandoned and left to Marty Budner to finish as a foreword — one thought dominated: no championship looks like Seaholm's Miracle Maples in Michigan's long love affair with high school sports.

The Maples endured a horrific 1987, the kind of season that can ruin a program or a coach's career. The first seed of the Miracle Maples was planted when Don Sackett called Mike Carroll in August of 1987. To me, this is the essence of high school sports. As stakeholders in our cities, we empower teachers and coaches to give our children some ownership in their schools. We fund clubs, bands and teams across a wide spectrum of activities. In sports, we print uniforms with a city or school name on the front and a family's surname on the back. We allow these young adults to represent our schools for a few hours on a Friday night. They run the plays in football, take the shot in basketball and pitch and hit in baseball. We let them represent our schools, win or lose. We make them available to the media when the games end.

When they fail, it's not always pretty, but there's always room for repair, and redemption. When taxpayers ask if it's all worth it, these life lessons are what we should all point to when we answer in the affirmative.

A year later, the Maples won it all, and the sheer improbability of it all remains striking. Winning five consecutive tournament games in their final turn at bat. Charging through Port Huron and Taylor Kennedy in the state finals. Eliminating five league champions. It's a remarkable pathway that's not been repeated. There have been other miracles. The Division 3 title won by Hillsdale in 2007 coming to mind quickly. Coach Chris Adams' team entered the state tournament with a record of 16-20 but rattled off seven consecutive wins and beat Beaverton, 8-6, to win a title no one thought they could. But Hillsdale didn't survive the same gauntlet the Maples faced, nor did they do it with the dramatic flair Seaholm did.

No Seaholm player was drafted. No player received a scholarship offer. No Maple was selected for the Class A Dream Team or First Team. In this context, the Miracle Maples stick out like a rusty pick-up truck rolling down an assembly line of brand new Mustangs.

On the day of the annual high school All-Star Game at Tiger Stadium, just days after winning the Class A title, *USA Today* named Seaholm No. 18 in their final, nationwide ranking. National lists like this were then a new fad and built upon balloting of high school and college coaches across the country. Often, they were derided by writers from daily metro papers. But to the Maples, who won 16 games in a row, lost just five times and upset two teams ranked in the top five, this was an important validation.

The 35 seniors on the field at Tiger Stadium that day included Avery, Gagin, Kimball's Siwajek and Berkley's Andy Fairman. Managing the team was Clouser, selected months ago to coach the game. Despite playing in what might have been the toughest league in the state and winning the Class A title in epic fashion, no Maple was selected to participate.

These slights mattered little to the town of Birmingham, smitten with their heroes. For the Maples, the summer was a three-month receiving line of handshakes, hugs and high fives, free ice cream cones and an occasional meal on the house. The city posted signs along its major roadways announcing Birmingham as, "Home of the Miracle Maples."

Avery signed his first pro contract on June 30 and was immediately sent to the Braves' Rookie League affiliate in Pulaski, Va. After 80 strikeouts and seven wins in 10 games, he was promoted to Class A, where he racked another 90 strikeouts in 13 games for the Durham Bulls.

In 1989, Seaholm didn't repeat as state champions, but they won the SMA for the first time in eight years and swept Kimball, eliminating their rival from the state tournament with a 17-9 drubbing in a pre-district game. Meanwhile Avery had already pitched 237 innings, racked 245 strikeouts and a 19-8 record in reaching Double-AA baseball in a little more than a full summer of work.

At the end of the spring of 1990, an era ended when Sackett announced he was retiring from teaching and coaching in Birmingham. Shades of another miracle appeared when Seaholm eliminated Lathrup and Dondero in the district, setting up a semifinal meeting with Clouser and Kimball.

The Maples trailed 5-1 in the sixth inning with just five outs to spare when they loaded the bases. A walk made it 5-2, and Ken Smith's single scored two more to make it 5-4. With the tying run just 90 feet away on the play, Kimball threw home to try and cut down the fourth run, allowing Smith, the potential winning run, to take second.

To everyone watching it unfold, it felt like the calendar had turned back to 1988.

But Clouser put a play on and his pitcher picked the tying run off third base. In the top of the seventh, they manufactured an insurance run before slamming the door on the Maples' last turn at bat to win, 6-4.

"I was standing right there, and that's how my career ended," Sackett said. "As a coach, I would never want my kid trying to pick off a player at third, because if the throw is bad, the run scores. But Clouser probably practiced that."

Sackett's Maples fall to Kimball at district

By Marty Budner
staff writer

It would have been so fitting for retiring Seaholm baseball coach Don Sackett.

Picture this scenario: The Maples rally to win their district baseball semifinal game over Royal Oak Kimball, then emerge with a big victory over regular-season Southeastern Michigan Association champion Berkley to claim the district title. Shades of 1988 and the Miracle Maple march to the Class A state championship.

But it wasn't to be.

Seaholm did stage a rally in its district semifinal against Kimball. But the Maples couldn't overcome some sloppy play and lost to the Knights, 6-4.

The game marked Sackett's final appearance in the maroon and white.

> 'We had some bad base running and made some errors. I hate to see my last game end like that. Things just didn't go our way today.'
>
> — Don Sackett
> Retiring Maple

Maple baseball uniform.

"We had some bad base running and made some errors. I hate to see my last game end like that," said Sackett. "But I have to give our team credit for coming back. Things just didn't go our way today.

"We knew we weren't going to win the league title, so our goal was to get to the districts. We beat a couple good teams — Lathrup and Dondero — to get here. That was a big accomplishment.

"We had a lot of rookies and a lot of inexperience out there today, and that inexperience is what hurt us in this game," Sackett said.

KIMBALL SPRINTED to the early lead, scoring twice in the first and twice in the third on singles by Tom Fuhrman and Jeff Young, and added another run in the fourth.

Seaholm scored once in the first on a base hit by Matt Faust which scored Jeff Hermanson. The Maples had runners picked off bases in both the second and third innings, and went scoreless over the next four innings and found themselves down 5-1 with just six outs left.

However, Seaholm staged a sixth-inning rally.

Craig Milius hit a one-out single, and Matt Faust, Justin Sweitzer and Eric Spencer each worked their way on with a walk to score Milius. Ken Smith then followed with a two-run single up the middle to make it a 5-4 game. The rally stalled at that point.

Kimball added an insurance tally in the top of the seventh. Seaholm put two runners on with one out in the bottom of the inning, but a pair of strike outs ended its season.

Paul Fleser didn't get much support and took the loss. The Maples finished with four runs on six hits, but made six errors and left eight men on base. Kimball wasn't that much better — the Knights had six hits, made four errors and left seven men stranded on the basepaths.

"We've played so many games over the years, and this was a typical Seaholm-Kimball game," said Sackett, whose team finished the season with a 10-11 overall record. "They're a bunt, and hit-and-run team, and that's what they did today. It's tough to beat them in close games.

"Basically our pitcher got behind on the count and he just didn't quite have it today," said Sackett. "You can't make mistakes like we did and expect to beat a team like Kimball.

"Our kids really wanted this game — and to their credit they hung in there for a while," he said.

JERRY ZOLYNSKY/staff photographer

Seaholm shortstop Matt Faust attempts to control the ball while Kimball's Tom Fuhrman (3) successfully swipes second during Saturday's district semifinal game at Memorial Field.

Don Sackett's final game ended up a 6-4 defeat to rival Kimball in the district semifinal, as reported by the *Observer & Eccentric*. The Knights' Jeff Harris would throw a no-hitter against Berkley to advance to another Class A regional.

A few hours later, Kimball won another district when Jeff Harris threw a no-hitter to beat Berkley, 1-0.

"I love my Dad. I learned a lot from him. But I'll never understand why he didn't spend 15 or 20 minutes every practice preparing for the things Kimball did," Mark Sackett said. "Seeing them twice a season and in the district, you have to wonder what his record might have been had he put more time into defending the unique things they did."

Sackett's baseball days were over but four days later, Avery's career began in Cincinnati, just six days past his 20th birthday. The Braves had rushed him to the big club — evidence his 3-11 record with a 5.64 record — but as one of the cornerstones of a budding dynasty, anything left to learn could be accomplished at the major league level. The media dubbed Avery, John Smoltz, Tom Glavine and Pete Smith the "Young Guns." Eventually, Smith would be replaced by Greg Maddux. In 1991, Avery was named Most Valuable Player of the National League Championship Series after winning a pair of 1-0 games, leading the Braves to the first of four pennants in six years.

Porter took over for Sackett in 1991 and almost immediately, experienced the same pressures Sackett did in facing Clouser.

"When I accepted the job, Seaholm's other coaches and teachers told me the program was usually pretty good, but they were also quick to point out we almost always lost to Kimball," Porter remembers. "Those first few years, the mental block was so real and so bad, I eventually decided to leave an extremely talented group of players together on sub-varsity — most of them were good enough to play on varsity — so they could experience beating Kimball, even if it was just freshman and junior varsity games. That changed everything and we no longer struggled against Kimball like we had."

In 1995, another era ended when Clouser resigned at Kimball. Earlier that season, Clouser's son hit his first career home run playing for Troy's freshman team, ironically against Kimball. When he learned of missing that moment later that evening, he informed Chuck Jones the following morning he would resign the position he'd held since 1969 at season's end.

That same year, Avery arrived at the pinnacle of his career, winning Game Four of the World Series, the only championship the Braves won during a 14-year stretch of winning the National League East every year (1991-2005). Just 25, Avery had logged 1,410.2 innings and 227 starts, 1,043 strikeouts and an 89-65 record in eight seasons of minor and major league service with Atlanta. Those totals were even more staggering because he only played half of 1988, and 1994-95 were plus shortened seasons due to labor disputes.

"Yeah, we pushed each other," Avery admitted to the *Atlanta Journal-Constitution* in 2014 when asked about his legacy with the Braves' Maddux, Glavine and Smoltz. "I think we went a couple years where we didn't even miss a start, which is unheard of."

Clouser re-appeared briefly on the coaching scene, following Mark Sackett at Troy Athens, coaching three seasons (1999-2001), winning 50 more games and two more league titles. He gave his former school a taste of what Seaholm endured, going 4-0 against Kimball. Clouser retired for good in 2001 with an overall record 596-240 (.713), part of a fraternity of 40 coaches in Michigan to have won at least 500 games in their coaching career.

It appeared Avery was done, too. He hadn't pitched since July 23, 1999, when surgery to repair a torn labrum below the rotator cuff ended his season. In three consecutive springs, Avery failed to make the Braves' Opening Day roster. A new opportunity arose in 2003 when Dave Dombrowski was named general manager in Detroit. The Tigers lacked significantly in talent and structural resources (scouting, player development, organizational direction, etc.) at the major league level and any help in Rookie, Short-A or Single-A baseball was years away from improving Detroit's major league product.

Intrigued by the possibility of bringing aboard a player who had pitched in four World Series, Dombrowski dispatched a pitching coach to watch Avery throw before signing him January 23. His contract was well north of the $100,000 he made as a rookie in 1990 with the Braves, but nothing close to the $4.85 million he reportedly made with the Boston Red Sox in 1997.

He didn't make the Tiger team out of spring training, but Avery was called up after 22 appearances in Toledo. Pitching in 19 games for the Tigers, Avery went 2-0 despite a 5.63 ERA, his true value the professional presence he offered on a team that came within a whisker of setting baseball's all-time season record for losses at 43-119 in 2003.

"I thought the world of Steve, and his ability spoke for itself," Dombrowski said. "He was someone who was local, who was a good guy, that we thought could help us bring the right attitude, right approach to the club, and he did that for us."

The 84 days of service Avery logged with the Tigers brought his major league service to 10 years and 25 days. After giving his best years to baseball at an incredibly young age, Avery was justly rewarded with full pension benefits, though it garnered little attention from the media.

Aside from the individuals within this title, the rivalries have largely disappeared from high school sports, too. The small leagues described in this title have been replaced by Sam's Club-sized conferences. The Oakland Activities Association and Macomb Area Conference combine anywhere from 20 to 40 schools into interchangeable divisions. Every two years, there's a schedule of promotion up or relegation down, much like English Premier League soccer, based on the success within the division and enrollment of the individual schools. It's entirely possible for the biggest division game to be played by two different schools on a yearly basis.

Week after week and month after month, the schedules roll by and few if any of the games are notable. Excitement doesn't ramp up until you advance far enough in the state playoffs, when it's often a one-off situation. Competing schools rarely build significant history with each other.

In many communities, the excitement of the big game on Friday night is gone, too. Camera phones and social media platforms have pushed our society's obsession with assigning knee-jerk blame to the highest-ranking school official whenever something goes wrong into hyperdrive. Commenters trying to publicly bully administrators into panicked decision-making is commonplace.

If principals and athletic directors own the risk of ensuring the safety and well-being of their students and staff — not to mention their own careers and future stability in retirement — what is their motivation to put any of it at risk by hosting bigger crowds?

So much has changed in high school athletics in the past 30 years, and I'm not sure for the better. But at Seaholm, athletic director Aaron Frank still tries to host as many Friday games as he can. Seaholm's role in the "Friday Night Lights" tradition and maintaining the connection between Seaholm and the Birmingham community it serves is, in Frank's mind, unwavering.

Seaholm's home football games continue to be a big draw within the Birmingham community. After last appearing in the state playoffs in 2012-13, the Maples returned in 2018. They're 5-0 against the new Royal Oak High School since Kimball closed in 2006. *(Hometown Life)*

"Most important, Friday home games mean our student-athletes aren't here at 10:30 p.m. on a school night, but Fridays are more fun and exciting," Frank says. "With the exception of games against Groves, the rivalries and big crowds don't exist for most of our teams. Football remains the one sport we pack the house for no matter who we're playing. I don't want to close the doors on our community to that unique experience."

The coach who serves for a quarter century or more at the same school is also an endangered species. Sackett and Clouser each coached 27 seasons at their schools. In the years following each man's retirement or resignation, nine coaches have followed, including six at Seaholm. From 1991-95, it was Greg Porter. He was replaced by Ron Hillier, who lasted just two weeks. Matt Newton took the reins in 1996-97. Pete Finn, now at Farmington, coached the Maples in 1997-99. Porter returned from 2000-05. Don Watchowski, Dan Drapel followed. Today, John Toth is at the helm.

Porter is the most successful of all Seaholm coaches to follow Don Sackett. In two separate stints, 1991-94 and 2000-04, Porter was 147-88 (.625). The head coach at Royal Oak since 2013, Porter is 117-53 (.688) entering 2019 with the Ravens.

In Royal Oak, it was Gordon as Kimball became Royal Oak High. Chris Lau followed when Gordon became athletic director, and in 2013, Porter became coach. Royal Oak's been more fortunate than most; at many high schools, the only constant seems to be the revolving door.

The Miracle Maples remain the only team in the 47-year history of the baseball tournament to win a district at Seaholm. It's a legacy the 1988 team struggles with.

"It seems like whenever I'm introduced in Birmingham, the person introducing me will say something like, 'Yes folks, he's one of the Miracle Maples,'" Carroll said. "Yes, we're proud we're the only team to have done it. At the same time, there isn't anyone on our team that wouldn't love to see Seaholm win another district, regional or state title."

Since retiring, Sackett and his wife have split time between a home in Michigan — with a spectacular view of the freighters passing along the Canadian shoreline on the St. Clair River — and a home in Florida. He still owns the car washes. Every week or so, Mark Sackett collects the canvas bags filled with quarters and deposits them into the bank.

As the 30-year anniversary approached, Seaholm hosted the team for a reunion. Almost a dozen former players came back to Birmingham, including Siefken from Colorado and Stephenson from Idaho. Sackett, now 85, still recalls the details of that historic season as if they happened last week.

Of the 15 Miracle Maples and four coaches from 1988, nine players and all the coaches returned for a 30-year reunion at Seaholm's doubleheader with Lake Orion. *Photo by Rocky Dennis*

"We had a big loss to Ferndale. We had a big win at Hazel Park. The doubleheader loss to Kimball was the low point of the season," Sackett said at the May reunion 30 years later. "But the end of the season was spread out, so we were able to play our best team, including our pitching in almost every game. That's why Newton went 11-1. "

And regarding Clouser and Kimball, Sackett remains deferential to his rival's legacy while getting a modest last laugh.

"You have to give Clouser his due; he was a great coach," Sackett said. "He wanted to win playing the bunt and squeeze plays — a very technical sort of guy with his bunt and sacrifice strategies — while I wanted our kids to have fun and swing the bat."

"He won and I lost more times than not when our teams played, but we won the same number of state championships."

More than anything, I hope *Miracle Maples* gave you a sense of what growing up in metro Detroit looked like 30 years ago. I hope it spoke to how the region as a whole has fought some awful battles regarding race and equality. Many communities have ended up on the wrong side of history in their fight to retain the status and citizenry they desired. I hope this title gave you a sense of the importance high school sports once held in these communities. If *Miracle Maples* told you who some of these young men were then, who they are now, and how the experience changed their lives, I've succeeded.

It would be easy to label this team with the usual stereotypes attached to Birmingham: rich, white and privileged. That perception didn't match what I learned about this team's reality. These Maples didn't drive new cars. They weren't trust fund kids, and they didn't stumble into a title they had no business winning. Their collective talent and resolve peaked at the exact moment necessary to pull off this epic feat.

Most of them lead simple, humble lives. Among them are accountants and attorneys, restaurant servers and contractors, property managers and military veterans. While some scattered across the country, they largely remain in Michigan. Some married, some remain bachelors, and some are divorced. They're brothers who have grown into roles as fathers and stepfathers, godparents and uncles. They now coach their own kids. For better and worse, in success and failure, this is their story, and I'm humbled by the responsibility of telling it all. It's part of Birmingham lore and Michigan's history.

Forever, they remain linked by the branches of this unique family tree, a legacy surmised by just two words.

Miracle Maples.

These iconic signs welcomed drivers to Birmingham at a handful of intersections, and one now hangs at Seaholm's home field. *Photo by Rocky Dennis*

APPENDIX NO. 1:

RETURNING COLGAN'S RING

AS A CHILD IN THE LATE 1980S, JIM ROSE TRAVELED BACK AND

forth regularly between his father in Lebanon, Indiana and his mother in Owensville, Missouri.

During one such trip, the path of Rose, an elementary school student, intersected with Crede Colgan, the recent Seaholm graduate. A championship ring changed hands that day. It would take 25 years before the ring reappeared.

Crede Colgan rarely played but was a memorable part of the Miracle Maples team because his powerful personality and sense of humor. *Photo by Dan Dean (Hometown Life)*

"I was making a trip down I-75, and I left my 'Miracle Maples' ring behind on a countertop while washing my hands at a rest stop," Colgan said. "I was in and out quickly, so it wasn't until I got to Florida that I realized I had left the ring behind."

Rose noticed the oversized prize on the counter. Grabbing the ring, he ran outside with his father in search of the owner. By the time they reached the parking lot, Colgan was speeding down the entrance ramp onto the interstate.

"We took the ring with us. I studied it, wondering how I could figure out who owned this prize," Rose said. "From time to time I would get it out and wear it around the house, pretending I had won some sort of game and was awarded this giant ring."

During a visit to Lebanon in 2013, Rose's father gave it back to Jim. Now an adult, Jim Rose was determined to make good on his promise.

"I thought I had lost it playing with it, and my father had wisely taken it knowing I would lose it," Rose said. "When he returned it I thought, 'Let's give it another shot and find the owner.'"

Rose first found the state, and then the school. When he landed on the Seaholm website, he found a link to the state championship, and was able to match the name on the ring with the name on the championship roster. During the Thanksgiving week of 2013, Rose contacted Colgan via email and arranged to return the ring.

To reciprocate, Colgan sent Rose a package of dinner and desserts from Omaha Steaks. It could not have come at a better time. Rose, who left Lebanon High School before graduating to take a job to help his family, had lost his job after many years of installing granite, quartz and marble countertops.

"His email was out of the blue, and I was overjoyed," Colgan said. "You lose something like this and figure you'll never get it back. I can't begin to explain how thankful I was."

CLOUSER FOLLOWS SACKETT

WHEN DON SACKETT RETIRED FOLLOWING THE END OF THE 1990

school year, Seaholm needed a new coach for the first time in 27 years. Sackett's son, Mark, wanted to follow in his father's footsteps.

"I naively believed I was most qualified," Sackett said. "I put a lot of stock in 1988, our first district and regional and state championship in program history."

Sackett wasn't considered. Instead, the job went to Greg Porter, who played at Central Michigan. Soon after, he named Don Righter as his junior varsity coach. Upset at being considered only for the freshman job, Sackett told Porter he would not to continue within the program.

It was a mistake.

"I thought two years playing at Michigan State University and five years as a varsity assistant should carry me further," Sackett said. "I arrogantly painted myself into a corner and had to look somewhere else."

Somewhere else was Troy High, where athletic director Dennis Seppanen gave Sackett a job. The freshman job.

"Mr. Seppanen was patient – tolerant would be a good word, too – of the mistakes I made as a young coach," Sackett says, "I started nine but played all nine of our substitutes and we had a fantastic season."

His 15-3 record earned Sackett the junior varsity job the next season. He continued to win, going 13-7 in 1992, 16-4 in 1993 and 18-3 in 1994. By the fall of 1995, with an overall record of 72-29 and Paul

Diegel locked into Troy's varsity job for the foreseeable future, Sackett applied for the varsity position at Troy Athens. He was named the school's new coach for the 1996 season.

Athens went 13-20 in 1996. Athletic director Doug Weaver retired and Bob Dowd, former head lacrosse coach at Detroit Country Day, took over as the new athletic director and assistant principal.

"Initially I related well with him, but Mr. Dowd did not agree with my expectation that unless you played a fall or winter sport at Athens, you participate in fall and winter baseball training," Sackett said.

Fall and pre-season training, now standard at every school's program, was a flap between Sackett and Dowd. In his determination to prove himself, Sackett began strangling the program instead of nurturing it slowly. The Red Hawks went 8-29 in 1997 and Dowd, who viewed baseball as a nuisance in the eyes of some, started to become intolerant of his young coach. As Sackett struggled and Athens continued to sag, things became more toxic. During a 1988 spring trip to Cincinnati, Sackett sent two players home for breaking team rules. With an 8-28 record that season and an overall mark of 29-77, Dowd asked for Sackett's resignation.

"Mr. Dowd said he would offer me a second chance after a few years," Sackett said, "but he had no intention of keeping that promise."

Dowd replaced Sackett with Clouser, who had most recently spent the previous two seasons as Diegel's assistant while his son, Andy, played for Troy.

Clouser called his three years at Athens, "the worst coaching experience of my life."

Figuring they knew of his past success, Clouser decided not to speak of his 27 seasons at Kimball when introducing himself to his new players.

"You should have seen the smirks on their faces when I told them I expected to win the league," Clouser said. "I knew right then it wasn't all Mark Sackett's fault they lost 28 games the year before. We had enough talent to win a state championship but the kids were screw-offs who didn't want to work hard. I didn't have a good athletic director, either."

Still, Clouser managed to win the OAA title in 1999 and 2000.

"On the last day of the 2000 season, Clouser beat me, 5-3, to win the OAA, and it was the only time I've ever had to console a coach who won a game to clinch the league title," said Porter, who went 147-88 (.625) in two stints at Seaholm (1991-94; 2000-04). "Frank was a Michigan high school baseball legend and he was miserable."

Since Athens, Sackett has served as managing director of the Michigan Red Sox since 2000, a 17-team youth organization with teams from 9U to 22U. He coached in the Great Lakes Collegiate League and the now-defunct Livonia Collegiate Wooden Bat League. He's had just one offer since Athens – Seaholm in 2006 – but after being offered the job, he declined in deference to his sons, Jay and James, who played on the varsity at Groves.

"I understand why (Seaholm athletic director) Aaron Frank was upset, but I couldn't coach against my kids," Sackett said. "Clouser waited for his son, Andy, to graduate from Troy, and I should have waited, too."

Does Sackett wish he'd stayed at Troy High School, coaching the junior varsity until Diegel left in early 2000's?

"Absolutely not. I wanted a varsity job and Athens gave me a chance," Sackett said. "Hopefully I'll get one more chance. It's never too late to make a positive difference."

1988 BIRMINGHAM SEAHOLM SCHEDULE AND RESULTS

Opponent	Result	Overall	League
Birmingham Groves (DH)	W, 7-0; W, 13-5	2-0	
West Bloomfield	W, 10-7	3-0	
Southfield	W, 7-0	4-0	1-0 SMA
Bloomfield Hills Lahser (DH)	W, 7-0; L, 7-3	5-1	
Troy	W, 13-3	6-1	2-0 SMA
Ferndale	L, 16-9	6-2	2-1 SMA
Hazel Park (DH)	W, 10-5; L, 4-0	7-3	3-2 SMA
Royal Oak Kimball* (DH)	L, 9-8; L, 8-1	7-5	3-4 SMA
Detroit Country Day	W, 6-1	8-5	
Troy	W, 8-6	9-5	4-4 SMA
Bloomfield Hills Andover (DH)	W, 13-5; W, 8-3	11-5	6-4 SMA
Berkley (DH)	W, 8-2; W, 9-6	13-5	8-4 SMA
Ferndale	W, 10-9	14-5	9-4 SMA
Southfield	W, 14-3	15-5	10-4 SMA
No. 2 Southfield Lathrup$	W, 3-2	16-5	
Birmingham Brother Rice	W, 2-1	17-5	
Troy	W, 3-2	18-5	
East Detroit@	W, 7-6 (9)	19-5	
Warren Mott#	W, 13-10 (8)	20-5	
Port Huron@	W, 7-2	21-5	
No. 5 Taylor Kennedy%	W, 11-9	22-5	

* Southeastern Michigan Association champion
$ Metro Suburban Athletic Association champion
# Macomb-Oakland Athletic Conference champion
@ Eastern Michigan League co-champion
% Tri-River League champion

BIRMINGHAM SEAHOLM MHSAA CHAMPIONSHIPS

Sport	Year(s)
Baseball	1988
Cross Country (Girls)	2012, 2014-15
Cross Country (Boys)	1959, 1963
Golf (Girls)	2006, 2008, 2013-15
Golf (Boys)	1958
Lacrosse (Girls)*	2007-09, 2011, 2012
Soccer (Girls)	1995
Swimming & Diving (Girls)	1995-97, 2016
Swimming & Diving (Boys)	1962-65, 2011, 2014-15
Track & Field	1933, 1936, 1937, 1942, 1949
Tennis (Girls)	1982, 2004, 2012, 2014-15, 2018

*won as Birmingham United, combining players from Birmingham Groves and Seaholm.

ABOUT THE AUTHOR

Miracle Maples is the fourth published title for author and journalist T.C. Cameron, a resident of Annapolis, Maryland since 2009. He worked at the *Capital-Gazette* newspapers from 2009-2015, covering high school and college sports at the United States Naval Academy. In 2017, he published Navy Football: Return to Glory from *The History Press*.

Cameron grew up in Royal Oak, Michigan — he's a 1988 graduate of Kimball — and holds a communications degree from Eastern Michigan University. He published Metro Detroit's High School Football Rivalries in 2008 and Metro Detroit's High School Basketball Rivalries in 2009. Both titles were from *Arcadia Publishing*.

Cameron has also officiated football, basketball and baseball at the high school and collegiate level in over a dozen states, for a handful of organizations, for over two decades.

He's an unabashed fan of the narrative found in sports writing.

Made in the USA
Monee, IL
20 November 2019